ANOKA COUNTY LIBRARY
707 HIGHWAY 10 N.E.
BLAINE, MN 55434-2398

D1116197

Clarice Cliff
and Her Contemporaries

Susie Cooper,
Keith Murray,
Charlotte Rhead,
and the Carlton
Ware Designers

Helen C.
Cunningham

4880 Lower Valley Road, Atglen, PA 19310 USA

Dedication

This book is dedicated with love
to my brother, Joseph Leslie Cartland, III.
He has always served as a steadfast reminder
of what is most important in life:
honesty, generosity, loyalty, kindness,
and consideration of others.
In addition, he taught by example
the importance of a logical approach,
which has served me well during my research.

Library of Congress Cataloging-in-Publication Data

Cunningham, Helen C.
    Clarice Cliff and her contemporaries: Susie Cooper,
    Keith Murray, Charlotte Rhead, and the Carlton Ware
    Designers/Helen C. Cunningham.
        p. cm.
    Includes bibliographical references and index.
    ISBN 0-7643-0706-1 (hardcover)
    1. Pottery, English--England--Staffordshire. 2. Pottery-
-20th century--England--Staffordshire. 3. Decoration and
ornament--England--Staffordshire--Art Deco. 4. Potters-En-
gland--Staffordshire--History--20th century. I. Title.
NK4087.S6C86   1999
738'.092'24246--dc21
                                        98-43306
                                        CIP

Copyright © 1999 by Helen C. Cunningham

All rights reserved. No part of this work may be reproduced or used in any form or by any means—graphic, elec-
tronic, or mechanical, including photocopying or information
storage and retrieval systems—without written permission
from the copyright holder.
    "Schiffer," "Schiffer Publishing Ltd. & Design," and the "De-
sign of pen and ink well" are registered trademarks of Schiffer
Publishing Ltd.

Designed by "Sue"
Type set in Beguiat Bk BT/Zurich BT

ISBN: 0-7643-0706-1
Printed in China
1 2 3 4

Title page photo:
A Charlotte Rhead jug depicting her *Persian Rose* design.
Collection of Carole A. Berke, Ltd.

Published by Schiffer Publishing Ltd.
4880 Lower Valley Road
Atglen, PA 19310
Phone: (610) 593-1777; Fax: (610) 593-2002
E-mail: Schifferbk@aol.com
**Please visit our web site catalog at
www.schifferbooks.com
or write for a free catalog**

This book may be purchased from the publisher.
Please include $3.95 for shipping.

In Europe, Schiffer books are distributed by
Bushwood Books
6 Marksbury Rd.
Kew Gardens
Surrey TW9 4JF England
Phone: 44 (0)181 392-8585; Fax: 44 (0)181 392-9876
E-mail: Bushwd@aol.com

Please try your bookstore first.

We are interested in hearing from authors
with book ideas on related subjects.

Contents

Acknowledgments

Without the cooperation of a great number of people, I could not have completed this most interesting project. First and foremost, I wish to thank Carole Berk of Carole A. Berk, Ltd., in Bethesda, Maryland. Carole immediately responded to my request for information and very graciously allowed me to photograph her wonderful selection of Clarice Cliff, along with other examples from the Art Deco period. Carole's shop includes a wide selection of Art Deco items, encompassing not only ceramic arts, but also jewelry, glassware, furniture, and silver. I very much appreciate her kindness and her willingness to share the collection with me. I also would like to thank Lisa M. Lertora for opening Carole's shop early one morning so that I could take the necessary photographs.

Others who have made this book possible include Constance and Richard Aranosian of *CARA Antiques. CARA Antiques* offers a variety of ceramic arts in addition to exciting examples of Clarice Cliff. They kindly allowed me to take photographs in their booth at the Southern Eagle Promotions, Inc. Antiques Show held in Atlanta, Georgia.

Andrew Plum of *Plum's Emporium* in Toronto, Canada, enthusiastically supplied information and photos for the chapter on Cooper. *Plum's Emporium* specializes in Susie Cooper. Thanks to him for his kind response and photographs.

As my quest for information continued, I was fortunate to meet with Helen and Keith Martin, owners of the *Carlton Ware Collectors International*, a club that meets annually in October in Stoke-on-Trent and also holds an international meeting outside of Great Britain. Here, club members meet with former Carlton Ware employees and attend lectures. In addition to the collectors' club, the Martins are premier British Carlton Ware dealers through their business, *St. Clere*. I am deeply indebted to them for all the kindness and hospitality they extended to me and to my husband on our research trip to England. Not only did the Martins allow me to photograph their extensive collection of Carlton Ware, but they also provided the majority of the historical information on the factory.

I was extremely fortunate to have the cooperation of Kathy Niblett of the *City Museum* in Stoke-on-Trent, England, as well. The *City Museum* is well worth a visit on any trip to England, as it houses some of the finest examples of British pottery to be found anywhere. I am very deeply indebted to Ms. Niblett for providing research information to me and for suggesting other sources where I might find the remaining data I needed. Her cooperation was key to much of the text herein. In addition, I am grateful to Miranda Goodby at the museum for her suggestions regarding people to contact. Also essential to my research was Mr. Peter Foden, Senior Archivist at the Stoke-on-Trent City Archives of the Hanley Library. Mr. Foden kindly allowed me to examine the factory records of A. J. Wilkinson and Newport Pottery, and also steered me to other sources.

Sharon Gater of the Wedgwood Museum in Stoke-on-Trent, England, was extremely gracious in allowing me to distract her from her duties as Research Assistant in order to give me a tour of the museum reserves where a delightful array of Cooper examples provided answers to many of my questions. I wish to extend my sincere gratitude to her for her valuable time.

I would also like to extend my thanks to Laurence Lattimore, whose World Wide Web page, *Lattimore's Art Deco Directory* at http://www.lattimore.co.uk/deco, proved invaluable. Laurie suggested a number of web pages that I should observe, and without his input, I surely would have missed some wonderful resources. Laurie specializes in Midwinter and other wares from the 1950s. Many thanks to him.

Jonathan Daltrey of *Banana Dance* specializes in twentieth-century decorative arts and he generously allowed me to photograph his booth at the Alexandra Palace Antiques Show in London. *Banana Dance* also has a web page on the World Wide Web: http://www.banana-dance.co.uk/banana.htm. Another important dealer whose help I genuinely appreciated is Lorraine Donnelly of *Lorraine Donnelly Art Deco Ceramics* on the Web at http://www.lattimore.co.uk/deco/donnelly. Lorraine kindly provided a number of photos for inclusion, as did F. V. Witney of *Witney & Airault* in Brighton, United Kingdom. The *Witney & Airault* World Wide Web address is http://www3.mistral.co.uk/witair.

Without the cooperation of Zoe Bajcer, whose shop, *May Avenue*, is located in the Antiquarius Antique Market in London, I could not have included some extremely rare examples of Clarice Cliff. Zoe was most cooperative and I am grateful to her. Zoe's web page address is www.mayavenue.co.uk. I also wish to thank Muir Hewitt of *Art Deco Originals* in Halifax, England, for his assistance and suggestions.

Other contributors include Nick Jones whose shop, *Susie Cooper Ceramics*, at Alfie's Antique Market in London, contains one of the largest collections of Cooper to be found anywhere. Nick graciously permitted me to photograph many important examples of Cooper found in his booth. Nearby is *Beverly*, whose shop offers a wide range of collectible ceramics. There, I obtained several needed photos. I was also fortunate to have the cooperation of Mark Markov and Peter Beedles of *Markov and Beedles*, specialists in Clarice Cliff Pottery at Sydney Street Antiques in London. Moreover, Carol C. Smith of *Grandad's Attic* in Aberdeen, Scotland, was most helpful. *Grandad's Attic* offers a nice selection of Cliff, Cooper, and other Art Deco ceramics.

Special thanks to fellow writers Marshall Katz, Nicholas Dawes, and John Bartlett. I am indebted to Marshall for immediately responding to my request for one of his many articles on pottery manufacturers, and to Nick and John for sharing sources of information with me. I also wish to thank Stephen Mullins of the *American Toby Jug Museum* in Evanston, Illinois, for his help in providing photos.

Thanks, too, go to Douglas Murray for his interest in this project and his constant enthusiasm about my pottery research. Also, I wish to extend my appreciation to Sam Jordan of Dury's Professional Photographic Supplies in Tennessee for his patience in answering all my questions related to photography.

My husband, Ben, and our children, Mera and Barrett, followed the progress of the project with keen interest and zeal. Their support and love kept me focused and enabled me to complete the manuscript.

Most importantly, I'd like to express my gratitude to Nancy and Peter Schiffer of Schiffer Publishing Ltd. I genuinely appreciate their trust and their cooperation, and I am delighted to have the good fortune of working with them and their fine professional staff. A special thanks, too, to the Design department and to my editor, Jennifer Lindbeck, who spent hours reviewing this manuscript. I genuinely appreciate her valuable assistance.

Preface

This book is intended as an introduction to several noteworthy pottery designers and manufacturers whose work establishes the parameters for twentieth-century pottery, beginning with the late 1920s. A number of very fine texts indeed already exist on Art Deco pottery, as well as inclusive texts on British pottery in general. In addition, there are a number of significant and noteworthy offerings on each of the designers and manufacturers included herein.

I do not intend for this book to compete with those already in print, but rather to complement them. I have attacked the subject of Art Deco and Modernist ceramics from an artistic standpoint, hoping to give the reader insight into why designers such as Clarice Cliff, Susie Cooper, Keith Murray, Charlotte Rhead, and those at Carlton have had a resurgence in popularity. Fundamentally, sound art will always have appeal, and these fundamentals are highlighted as a part of my approach. Since I have chosen to study the pottery from an artistic as well as a historical viewpoint, I feel it is important to include close-ups of the design details where necessary. Clarice Cliff, for example, wanted her designs to have visible brushstrokes, so it is essential that the reader be provided with detailed photos showing the strokes. Charlotte Rhead's tube-lined designs also require close-up photos to understand the intricate patterns. I hope this book will serve as an introduction for new and not-so-new collectors of period pottery and act as a springboard for further research.

My interest in these designers began over ten years ago when I first noticed Clarice Cliff's ceramics. I stumbled upon an entire booth displaying the brightly decorated wares designed by Cliff at an art pottery show, and her designs piqued my curiosity. These wares stood in stark contrast to much of the early twentieth-century art pottery, and I became curious about the designer. Did the designer have a personality as outgoing as her designs would indicate? Why did she choose to decorate with such wonderful yellows, oranges, reds, blues, and greens? How did she work? On what did she base her designs? Having been a collector of nineteenth and early twentieth-century pottery for over twenty years (my last book entitled *Majolica Figures*), I knew the artistry and stamina required to produce anything new in the world of ceramics. Quite familiar with the art history of the period, I began to make connections and this book developed.

Once I began to research Clarice Cliff, it was impossible not to explore her contemporaries. Susie Cooper contrasts nicely with Cliff, not only in personality and background, but in her approach to design. Cooper's technically skilled lithographs contrast Cliff's hand-painted designs. Even when Cooper began creating freehand designs, she limited her use of color to only a few subtle ones, unlike Cliff's bold reds and yellows. Both as women and designers, Cliff and Cooper established a place for themselves in history, not only because of their wonderful creativity and unique approach to ceramics, but also because they directed manufacturing plants when women were rarely in positions of authority. In fact, during that time, women had only recently gained the right to vote! These women set examples for other women to follow, not only in the field of ceramics.

Such is also the case with Charlotte Rhead. Her elegant designs differ from Cliff's and Cooper's. Despite coming from a family of pottery designers, Charlotte's patterns nonetheless only recently attracted the attention of collectors on both sides of the Atlantic.

Because of the number of factories in the Stoke-on-Trent area during the late nineteenth and early twentieth centuries, the area is frequently referred to simply as "The Potteries." Beehive kilns dot the horizon.

In addition to the women designers mentioned, Keith Murray should also be included in a study of twentieth-century pottery. Murray began his career as an architect, and it is this architectural approach that he used in designing his pottery. His unique creations contrast the colorful patterns of Cliff and Rhead, and the delicate ones of Cooper.

To round out the era, I felt that Carlton Ware offered the most variety and would add depth to any text on twentieth-century pottery. The designers at the Carlton factory quickly adapted to any change in fashion. This remarkable ability to notice a trend and act upon it makes Carlton one of the most interesting to collect because of its wide range of styles. Many collectors choose to specialize in a particular item, color, design, or period. Others collect a sampling of different styles by Carlton Ware.

While there are many other manufacturers and designers that could be included, I feel that the ones I have chosen to include highlight the wide range of styles and designs offered during the period. In keeping with the study of British ceramics, the English spellings of words are used when quoting or using names. Otherwise, the American spellings are used. Examples include "grey" rather than "gray," "modelling" as opposed to "modeling," "coloring" with a "u," "matt" instead of "matte," and "lustre" rather than the American spelling of "luster."

By way of explanation for those unfamiliar with the geography of Britain, Staffordshire is an area northeast of London. Six Staffordshire towns actually comprise the city called Stoke-on-Trent, which lies about two hours from London and one hour from Manchester. These six towns include Burslem, Fenton, Hanley, Longton, Stoke, and Tunstall. Beehive kilns dotted the landscape at the turn of the twentieth century; consequently, the area was often referred to simply as The Potteries. Today, the region still relies heavily on the pottery industry with the Royal Doulton, Spode, Minton, Moorcroft, and Wedgwood factories in production, along with numerous "factory shops" or outlets scattered throughout the area. In addition, the wonderful City Museum and Art Gallery, as well as the Gladstone Museum, offers visitors insight into the history of the area and the pottery production. For serious pottery enthusiasts, The Potteries is well worth any detour on a trip to England.

Pricing Information

The prices contained herein offer a range and are intended only as a general reference. Prices quoted are in U. S. dollars. Although the range is derived from actual selling prices, both in shops and at auctions, prices are always affected by condition, coloring, detail, size, rarity, and, above all, collectibility. For example, the rarest designs sometimes bring lower prices simply because they are not as collectible. Very often the rarest pieces sell below value simply because they are not common enough to be recognized, so collectors will pass over them in favor of the more recognizable designs. Sometimes these more common examples bring far beyond their value for the same reason: they are familiar.

I have attempted to offer an average price range for pieces in very good condition. Exceptionally mint pieces will realize higher prices. While chips or minor damage should not deter the collector from buying a piece, these should be clearly reflected in the price. Whenever possible, it is best to buy pieces that are as near to perfect condition as the budget will allow. However, some pieces are so rare that damage is overlooked. A few photos are included in the text to illustrate this point and no price is available; these have "NP" in the caption, meaning "no price." Groupings also have no price indicated, since they are included to show a range or collection and not a specific piece. Other pieces may have 'NP" indicated because no price was available.

Pottery prices are always variable. In general, they are rising steadily, especially on the better pieces. At any given time, however, it is difficult to put a definitive price on any piece of pottery. I feel that a price range will give collectors a better idea of the relative values for a piece. Remember that the prices quoted are retail prices. If selling or buying wholesale, the price should be about half of these prices. Dealers spend a great deal of time obtaining pieces and have a great deal of expenses. They must receive compensation for their time, effort, and knowledge. Never begrudge a dealer his or her profit. They have earned it! Moreover, do not expect a dealer to pay the price quoted in this guide.

Prices, of course, vary according to the section of the country, and even the country itself. Furthermore, the concentration of collectors effects prices. It follows that prices are higher where demand is higher. These British designers and factories have attracted the attention of collectors on both sides of the Atlantic. Demand for the ceramics included in this book still remains high and continues to rise in Britain, and, as more and more collectors enter the field, demand and prices are steadily rising in the United States. However, enough pieces are available for a variety of budgets that the beginning collector as well as the advanced collector can hope to increase his or her collection.

For the sake of the collector, the items in this book are arranged in categories, and a price range is given for each category. The higher end of the price range is broader, as there is more variability in price. Within each category, I indicate where a particular design falls. If the design falls at the lower end of the category price range, the word "Low" appears in the caption. For example, *Crocus* designs were among Clarice Cliff's most successful, so the pattern was produced for a long period of time. Pieces in this design are generally available. Items of this pattern generally fall in the lower end of the respective category price range. For items at the middle or the high end of the price range, I have marked "Medium" or "High" respectively. Pieces that average above a given range will have a "+" included. Inevitably, when giving a price range, there is some overlap. In addition, some pieces are rare or hard to find; this is also indicated. Designs that are at the lower end of the price range may be a good starting place for beginning collectors, as these pieces are generally more available. Advanced collectors are probably searching for the harder to find items.

Rather than buying an example because it represents a "good buy," a collector should buy what he or she loves. As a pottery collector for more than twenty years, I have found that more and more I buy pieces because they "speak to me," meaning I find them aesthetically satisfying, artistically balanced, and carefully crafted. If the lines and proportions are "right," and the piece is well-constructed and has eye-appeal, more than likely it will go up in value. Today's bargains may become tomorrow's disasters. By buying what truly appeals to the soul, the collector can enjoy and appreciate the piece for years to come. As collectors upgrade their collections, they will find that the pieces they were drawn to for good sound reasons will also appeal to others.

Over the years, I have found that good pieces make better investments. In general, try to buy pieces in the best condition affordable. Damaged pieces usually do not increase in value as much over the years as mint pieces. However, damage is often overlooked on rare items or items known as "shelf pieces;" these pieces collectors desire to complete a particular portion of the collection or to "round out" the range.

Introduction

Setting the Stage

In the early nineteenth century, Britain's geographical position and ample natural resources put her in an enviable position as the Industrial Revolution began. The economic strength encouraged a pride in industry, which resulted in a rise in industrialization that helped create more than just two classes. Prosperous merchants established an ever-increasing middle class. The new "bourgeoisie" at first copied the aristocracy, but gradually began to develop a taste on its own. The century witnessed one revival after another as the rising middle class sought to display its new wealth. Libraries and newspapers enabled the growing middle class access to information and educational opportunities that had been denied them in previous centuries.

An elite society no longer existed, but there now was a middle class lacking in self-confidence as far as style was concerned. It lacked the standards necessary for judging art and culture; consequently, consumers immediately latched onto each new fashion trend lest they be considered out of step with style. While manufacturers tried to stay ahead of the demand for new designs, the vast majority of nineteenth-century, middle-class homes filled with factory-made knickknacks. This frenzied desire to display newfound wealth created eager consumers.

By the last quarter of the nineteenth century, Britain began losing her position of dominance in world trade. The prosperity of the first half of the century slowed. Lifestyles and attitudes became less restrictive. As the reaction to manufactured goods began to swell, the Arts and Crafts Movement began. By the end of the First World War, the restrictions created by the socially insecure middle class began to loosen. The new century witnessed more stylistic independence and autonomy. The rigid social structures lessened as the middle class gained confidence. Cultural regimen was replaced with an enlivened attitude. The artistic experimentation begun by the Impressionist painters in the last quarter of the nineteenth century perhaps inspired consumers and artists alike to explore. The new century witnessed the development of Art Nouveau, which ultimately led to the Art Deco and then Modernist styles. By examining the products and manufacturers prior to the Art Deco period, as well as the manufacturers that directly competed with Clarice Cliff and her contemporaries included in this text, the collector will gain a clearer picture of the social context in which these designers created.

Chapter One
Stylistic Trends in the Arts

Impressionism and Postimpressionism

Impressionism began in 1874 when a group of artists held an exhibition of their work which the Salon in Paris had rejected. These new artists painted everyday subjects without pretense. For the first time, the middle class became subjects of art. The Impressionists such as Cézanne created imaginary landscapes and increased the range of colors used as they worked to capture on canvas the varying effects of sunlight during different times of the day.

By 1895, another movement in art arose. Unlike the emphasis the Impressionists placed on how one sees the world, the Postimpressionists emphasized one's understanding of it. Postimpressionism is a hybrid term used to categorize the artistry of the last fifteen years of the nineteenth century. Artists of the period sought to express their world as they saw it in their minds and as their feelings interpreted it. They turned from the haze of breezy brush strokes that typified the Impressionist paintings to curving lines with strong colors: characteristics that led the way for the Art Nouveau movement.

Even as poets sought music to go with their verse, the Postimpressionist artists acknowledged music as inspiration to them also. Musicians added poetry to their music. Strauss incorporated natural sounds into his tone poems, while musicians such as Debussy expressed the subtlety of the Impressionists' paintings in symphonies. This background indeed affected the Art Nouveau movement, as it sought to encompass all of the arts.

The Japanese Influence

Interest in *Japonisme* began when Commodore Matthew Perry, a United States naval commander, secured a formal trade agreement with Japan in 1854. After that time, Japanese products became available both in Europe and America.

Prior to Perry's visit, Japan had isolated itself, so these new designs immediately caught the attention of the consuming public on both sides of the Atlantic.

Japanese wares were included in the South Kensington International Exhibition of 1862 and the Paris Exhibition of 1867. The restrained, formal lines of the Japanese motifs also influenced the pottery of the period. Although the pottery retained its western shapes, small sprays of flowers inspired by Japanese designs decorated it. Simple asymmetrical designs appeared on basketweave or bamboo backgrounds.

A reaction to mechanization at the end of the nineteenth century witnessed an attraction to more natural lines. As early as the mid-nineteenth century, John Ruskin had sought true beauty through a return to real craftsmanship. William Morris, a friend of Ruskin, established the Morris & Company to enable skilled workers to practice their art and not be forced to toil in factories. This way the average home could appreciate true beauty, not mass produced knick-knacks.

From the Arts and Crafts Society William Morris founded in 1888, the Arts and Crafts Movement started. The Morris & Company created a collaboration of the arts. Pre-Raphaelite painters such as Burne-Jones and Rosetti decorated furniture. Natural designs inspired the Morris style. The use of organic lines and harmonious effort foreshadowed the later style of Art Nouveau. The rise in popularity of Art Nouveau, with its curving lines and elegant detail, seemed a natural outgrowth of the Postimpressionists' ideas as well. Art Nouveau quickly spread in the decorative arts.

The Art Nouveau Style

The Art Nouveau style was first exhibited in 1889 and again at the 1900 Universal Exhibition in Paris. The idea of combining the arts as the Postimpressionists had done appealed to the late Victorian craftsman. Literature and music served as inspirations for craftsmen like Émile Gallé who inscribed quotations or poems on his glassware and furniture.

First appearing in England, the sinuous lines spread rapidly throughout Europe. The terms for this new style varied in each country: from "Art Nouveau" to "Modern Style" in France, "Stile Liberty" and "Moderne Stile" in Italy, and "Modernismo" in Spain. It was not until 1905 that the style began to decline.

Art Nouveau is obviously reminiscent of Japanese art, which emphasizes flat, delicate patterns without much ornamentation and on a plain background. In fact, the term itself is named after the Parisian shop opened in 1895 by the German emigrant Samuel Bing. Bing, who had been trading in Japanese art for ten years, wanted to expand his shop to include a gallery and a showroom. He commissioned painters, sculptors, and designers for his shop. Bing's success in combining the decorative arts and designs with fine art in his shop, "La Maison de l'Art Nouveau," gave him the opportunity to exhibit at the Paris Exposition Universelle of 1900. He was even allotted an entire pavilion!

Although it was Bing who was recognized as the impresario of Art Nouveau (a term only used by collectors in hindsight to describe the style), it was Arthur Mackmurdo's Century Guild that first put forth the sinuous forms with their flowing lines. The Century Guild, as a member of the Arts and Crafts Exhibition Society, retained the ideas of William Morris and the Society. Mackmurdo elongated the shapes and made the patterns more elegant, thus becoming the first to embody the characteristics of Art Nouveau and originate the concept of merging rippling, sinuous lines with slender, asymmetrical shapes, and stylized forms.

The Turn of the Century and Expressionism

The restrictions of the Victorian era gave way to more freedom as the new century dawned. The trend toward experimentation in the arts that had begun in the last quarter of the nineteenth century continued into the twentieth. The arts, perhaps influenced by the Postimpressionists and their emphasis on feelings, responded to the need for freedom of expression. Dancers like Isadora Duncan improvised to music by Saint-Saëns. She emphasized free-flowing movements based on emotional responses to music rather than the unnatural structure of ballet. Thus began modern dance. Duncan and her followers danced barefoot in loose, gauzy attire rather than "en pointe" in tight, restrictive tutus.

Not only was change obvious in dance, but in art as well. Expressionism was a term first used by a German critic in 1911 to capture the essence of the art produced by the Fauvists and Cubists as well as other modernist painters. Their art was both intense and emotional. The earlier Postimpressionist's like Gauguin and Van Gogh had painted emotional subjects in abstract forms with intense colors. The Expressionists continued the emotionalism begun by their predecessors, depicting in their art their emotional response to the world around them. They tried to paint their reaction to their environment.

The geometrical style of the Cubists like Picasso and Braque would not have developed without the spatial forms of Cézanne. Fauvist painters like Matisse were inspired by Van Gogh's emotional emphasis and Gauguin's dimensions. The Fauvists, meaning "wild beasts," stressed expressive use of color to create the illusion of three dimensions.

Cubism

Juxtaposed to Expressionism was Cubism. Georges Braque and Pablo Picasso are credited with creating the Cubist style, though they themselves never used the term. Influenced by African art imported from the European colonies and by the artistic planes of Cézanne, these two painters created abstract works based on geometric shapes. The African masks that hung on the walls of these artists' studios conveyed emotionalism in a realistic, yet at the same time, abstract way. Much like the Japanese influence in the late 1800s, the importation of primitive examples strongly influenced the arts. Moreover, Cézanne's spatial planes seemed to inspire the artists to envision an object from many angles at the same time. By delivering these ideas in neutral colors, Cubism began.

In 1907, the first phase of Cubism, called Analytic Cubism, surfaced. Tilting planes gave as many perspectives as possible at the same time. Picasso commented: "Of course, when I want to make a cup, I'll show you that it is round, but the overall rhythm of the painting, the structure, may force me to show this roundness as a square." He later commented that "art makes us realize the truth."[1]

By means of restricted palettes and parallel, diagonal lines, Cubist painters created faceted figures in space using varying planes. Analytic Cubism, beginning to wane by 1912, had forced the viewer to consider these different planes as an abstract representation of the real world. By the early 1920s, Cubism followed other art forms in seeking new perspectives, and Synthetic Cubism was the result. "Synthetic" implied creating something new, something unnatural. Thus, Synthetic Cubism created a new reality, not by breaking up shapes, but by bringing them together. This kind of Cubism assembled arbitrary, two-dimensional pieces of the real world into a new representation. Experimentation and altering perspectives affected not only the art world, but the ceramic world as well. These artists and their successors directly influenced the artistic endeavors of the ceramic designers of the period. One needs only to observe Braque's *House Behind Trees* to discover Clarice Cliff's inspiration for a number of her designs. The tree in the foreground forces one to focus on the tree, yet still observe the cottage in the background, providing a depth of perspective. Several of Clarice Cliff's designs utilize this concept.

Besides Picasso and Braque, others began experimenting with Cubism. The Dutch artist Piet Mondrian lived in Paris during the waning years of Analytic Cubism. It was Mondrian who attempted to express emotions through the use of two-dimensional, rectilinear shapes and a balance of primary colors. Because he disliked curves, all of Mondrian's lines were straight. His use of bright yellows, reds, and blues carefully complemented his use of black rectangles and lines. It was this arrangement of black lines intersecting blocks of bright colors that must have intrigued not only Clarice Cliff, but Susie Cooper and Charlotte Rhead as well. Their telltale use of black to attract the eye and draw the eye upward and outward might very well be traced directly to Mondrian.

Constructivism and Futurism

As Cubist painters began adding other materials to their artwork, collages developed. Following the addition of letters to their paintings, Picasso and Braque experimented with the addition of sand, rope, wood, caning, and a variety of unusual items to their artwork. This Constructivism, as it came to be called, encouraged the Russian Vladimir Tatlin to use sheet metal in one of his paintings. Another artist incorporated a tire into one of his paintings. Constructionists opposed the Aesthetics' concept of 'art for art's sake,' a phrase coined by French philosopher Victor Cousin in his lectures at the Sorbonne in 1818, which represented the focus of art since the mid-nineteenth century.

Besides the Russians' adaptation of Cubism, the Italians created yet another dimension. Some Italian artists combined Impressionism and Cubism and called it Futurism. Futurism focused on intense movement. For example, speeding machines such as racing automobiles, or rioting crowds, became apt subjects for the Futurists. Seeing all stages of motion at once related an immediacy they felt other art styles were lacking.

Also influenced by Cubism was a Romanian sculptor named Constantin Brancusi. He began to emphasize natural shapes and forms like those of leaves and eggs. His attention to detail and elemental designs started a movement toward streamlining art. One of Brancusi's most famous creations is a simple 96-foot zigzag tower entitled *Endless Column*. Perhaps Brancusi and his followers are as important as other Cubists in their impact on the Art Deco designers. His use of zigzags along with his appreciation of natural elements certainly must have inspired Susie Cooper, as well as Clarice Cliff and Keith Murray. Streamlined offerings indeed set the stage for the modern lines of the 1950s. Moreover, the appreciation of nature may have set the stage for the emphasis on the female form which became so popular in the Art Deco period.

Amadeo Modigliani, an Italian who moved to Paris during the incipient stage of Cubism, created sculptures influenced by Brancusi as well as African art. Later, he turned to paintings of women with elongated faces and necks. Modigliani's designs perhaps inspired some of Clarice Cliff's designs, particularly her *May Avenue.*

Dada and Surrealism

After World War I, Cubism, along with its disciples Constructivism and Futurism, declined as Dada and Surrealism entered the scene. The antisocial aspects of these bizarre paintings attracted the attention of the public. Dada made art by combining everyday, mundane objects. Surrealism, in contrast, utilized free association as a means of tapping the unconscious. Inspired by Sigmund Freud, the Surrealists mixed imagination and abstraction. Both Dada and Surrealism were highly experimental styles. The years between the wars were gloomy and haunting, a critical time for artists. Fantasy perhaps offered a diversion.

Joan Miró, a Spanish artist, suggested feelings by quick use of lines and dots. Another Surrealist, Salvador Dali, used the canvas to capture his dreams. Marc Chagall illustrated his bizarre, badly proportioned figures in bright colors. The whimsical, fantasy-based paintings of the Surrealists unlocked the subconscious and freed the spirit, something that was to stand the creative genius of the upcoming ceramic designers in good stead.

Art Deco and the Ceramic Arts

The *Exposition des Arts Décoratifs et Industriel* in Paris in 1925 led to the naming of the period between the wars as Art Deco. Although the term was not applied until the 1960s, the term seemed appropriate since the period followed Art Nouveau. Like its predecessor Art Nouveau, Art Deco also focused on lavishness. Fine materials and excellent craftsmanship exemplify both periods. Although actually originating before World War I, Art Deco is traditionally associated with the period after the war.

With its roots in Cubism, Russian Constructivism, and Italian Futurism, Art Deco is at once abstract, simple, and very stylized. Geometric designs, such as zigzags and chevrons, stylized women and bouquets of flowers, and the omnipresent streamlined doe typify the period. The Art Deco style sought to combine the unexpected: black, lacquered wood with metal (usually steel) and rounded rather than square corners.

The original Art Deco designers catered to select patrons. The emphasis on fine craftsmanship and materials was expressed in "limited editions," an idea that contrasted with the later modernist's appreciation for the benefits of commercialism. Because Modernists felt that mass produced items also could reflect quality, they perfectly adapted wares for their intended purposes, conforming pieces so form followed function. Early Art Deco designers emphasized handcrafted items. However, in order to attract the consumer, pottery manufacturers combined the two concepts: advertising their products as "hand-painted" or naming a range "Handcraft." Though mass produced for the average consumer, these manufacturers sought to align themselves with the early tenants of the Art Deco style.

The Superintendent of the Schools of Art in The Potteries area of Staffordshire, Gordon Forsyth, felt that only through art could the pottery industry add a new dimension to its products. Not every pottery manufacturer agreed with him, however. Many felt that the "Jazz Modern" movement, a term they used disparagingly, placed too much emphasis on design. According to an article by Cyril Carter of Carter, Stabler & Adam's Pottery in the *Pottery Gazette & Glass Trade Review,* Mr. Forsyth's opinion caused manufacturers to emphasize art and not "honest pottery fitting in every way for the purpose for which it is made."[2]

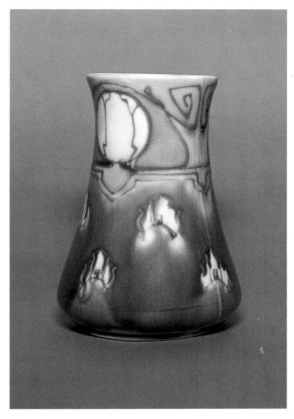

These Minton vases from around the turn of the nineteenth century foreshadow the interest in the use of black lines as an integral part of the design. Clarice Cliff utilized striking black lines as a contrasting element in many of her most famous designs. *Collection of Carole A. Berk, Ltd.* NP

Art Deco declined after World War II when modern, streamlined wares appeared on the market. The war-weary consumer sought something new and different, something fresh and unencumbered. It was not until the 1970s that a revival of the Art Deco styles began. Today, there remains an increasing interest in the phenomenon known as Art Deco.

This Minton *Secessionist* cheese dish from the turn of the nineteenth century suggests the tube-lining concept that became popular in the 1930s and 1940s. *Courtesy of CARA Antiques.* NP

These Doulton pieces indicate the developing concepts that were used by many of the Art Deco designers: stylized fruit and flowers or geometric shapes. *Collection of Carole A. Berk, Ltd.* NP

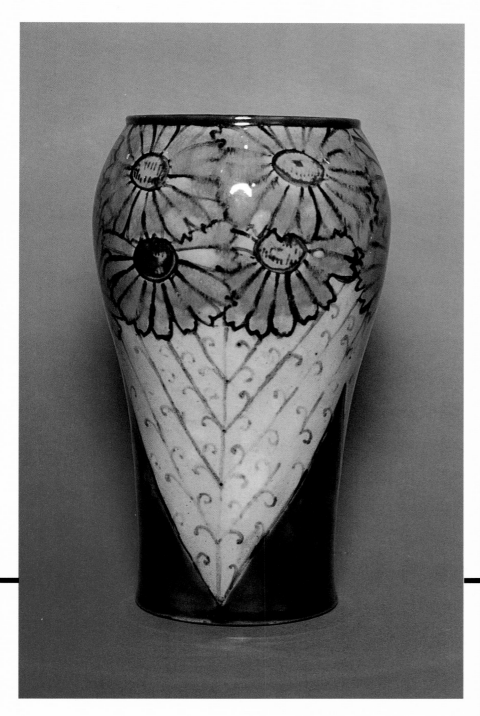

Designers in the field of ceramic arts have always experimented with new concepts, constantly creating unusual products. For example, these Doulton jugs from the turn of the nineteenth century appear to be made of leather and copper, yet they are ceramic. The designers of the Art Deco period perhaps inherited the creative passions of their ancestors, for they, too, constantly searched for new and fresh ideas. NP

As the Deco years approached, orange became an important color, seen here on a Royal Lancastrian vase and the Czech glass vases. *Collection of Carole A. Berk, Ltd.* NP

The Postwar Years and Modernism

Precursors of abstract art began with the juxtaposing of colors, shapes, and patterns in paintings like those by Cézanne. One plane or contour is interrupted by another that seems to overlap it. These ideas led to Abstract Expressionism and later to Modern Art. Abstract Expressionism expressed feelings with its vibrating, pulsating use of color. The term itself, like most other labels for artistic styles, was coined by an art critic. Not all critics agreed, however. Some felt that the art was neither abstract or expressive. The artists of the 1940s felt the term inappropriate. Somewhat akin to earlier Expressionism, these painters wanted to discover a universal truth or memory.

Growing out of Cubism and Surrealism yet rooted in the Great Depression, the Abstract Expressionist movement is typified by large, abstract splashes of color. Originally begun as a social protest, Abstract Expressionism was an American movement based on the European styles. By the 1950s, the developing style became synonymous with the

American individualism of the Cold War era. America was now replacing Europe as the center of the art world.

Other art movements, such as Pop Art, Minimalism, Conceptualism, and Postmodernism, developed as the "modern" era focused on commercial success. The Postwar years were bleak and drab. Pop (short for populist) art celebrated mass production and everyday life by using commercial items. For Pop artists, items like soup cans in large quantities stood as a symbol of opposition to the individualism so respected by the Abstract Expressionists. For the first time, artists became mainstream and more public in its orientation. Art appeared in front of libraries and businesses and more and more consumers managed to afford artistic pieces.

Compare the flowing lines, subtle colors, and high shoulders on this Arts and Crafts vase . . . *Courtesy of David Lyle and Douglas Murray.* NP

The 1950s witnessed a loosening of the wartime restrictions and allowed for subtle colors and unusual shapes. Corners became rounded, reminiscent in some ways of the Art Deco period. Edges lost their rims and streamlined forms appeared. Elongated and smooth, atypical shapes with random designs offered variety to the no longer deprived consumer.

In contrast, the hippies of the 1960s and 1970s celebrated their lifestyle with a brash boldness heretofore unseen. Their love for bright colors and their emphasis on naturalism inspired artists and designers. Fundamental geometric shapes, often in shades of brown, reappeared as a basis for design. In addition, avocado green and harvest gold were popular colors of the 1970s.

. . . to the sloping shoulders and bright colors of this Wilkinson *Tahiti* vase. *Collection of Carole A. Berk, Ltd.* NP

In France, designers like Barol combined the stylized flowers and incised lines with black highlights exhibiting the important concepts of Art Deco ceramics. This wall plaque dates from 1917 to 1921. NP

In the 1980s, black lines, similar to those on the later Cubist art, began to reappear. Black had disappeared as a color of design for several decades. Other popular colors included navy with pastels such as mauves and soft blues. The later designs by Susie Cooper as well as many of the later Carlton Ware designs show influence of these trends.

In conclusion, collectors must seek to understand the contributions of designers like Clarice Cliff, Susie Cooper, Charlotte Rhead, Keith Murray, and those at the Carlton factory, in light of the artistic heritage that affected and inspired their creations. These artisans crafted some of the freshest, yet most enduring, patterns on the market. Among these designers, there is truly something to attract everyone!

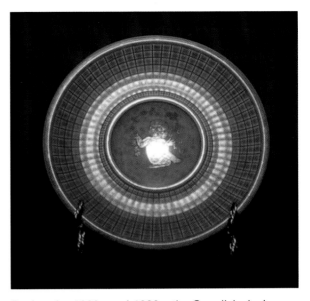

During the 1920s and 1930s, the Swedish designers of Gustavsberg focused on elegant yet simple shapes with silver overlay designs. This particular example uses complementary incised squares on a circular shape. NP

Three Poole Pottery examples from southern England illustrate the focus on hand-painted flowers, wonderful color combinations, and full, rounded shapes popular during the Art Deco period. *Collection of Carole A. Berk, Ltd.* NP

Honiton was another manufacturer from the south of England. This pitcher displays a soft yellow body similar to that of many Clarice Cliff designs. NP

An array of Art Deco pitchers and vases exhibit the variety of shapes available during the Art Deco years. *Courtesy of Witney & Airault (Decorative Arts).* NP

This Burleigh Ware pitcher combines several shades and tones of yellow. *Courtesy of Witney & Airault (Decorative Arts).* NP

These Burleigh Ware pitchers illustrate the primary colors often used in English Art Deco ceramics. During this period, English manufacturers offered brightly colored wares to compete with the cheaper ones imported from Czechoslovakia. *May Avenue, Antiquarius, London.* NP

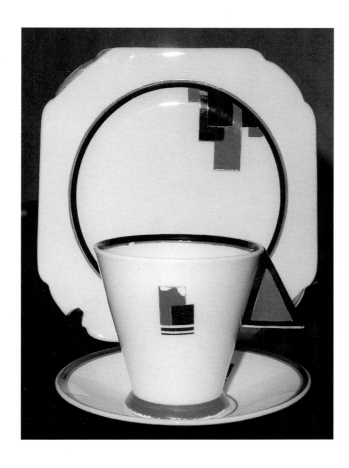

Far left and left:
Art Deco manufacturers created not only interesting color combinations but interesting shapes as well, like these teaware sets from Shelley Potteries. Compare these sets to those by Clarice Cliff and Carlton Ware. Appropriately named *Mode*, the red and black design appeared on the market in 1930. *Courtesy of Lorraine Donnelly Art Deco Ceramics*. NP

Besides the colors of this figure, the elegant lines and tilting head are indicative of figures from the Art Deco period. *Courtesy of Witney & Airault (Decorative Arts)*. NP

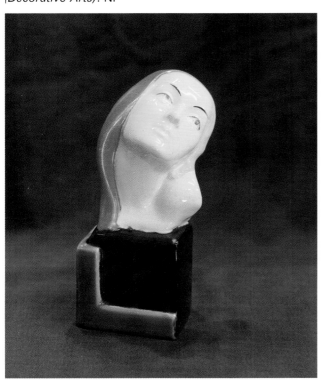

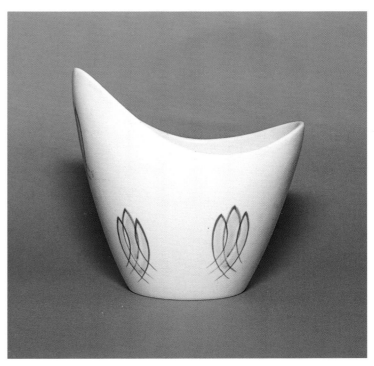

After the end of World War II, an interest in streamlined shapes typified the modern movement in decorative arts. Ceramics, of course, was no exception. This Poole Potteries vase is typical of the trend. *Collection of Carole A. Berk, Ltd*. NP

Chapter Two

Clarice Cliff

How Bizarre a Beginning . . .

Born in January of 1899 to a Staffordshire family, Clarice Cliff was the fourth of eight children. Her father was an iron molder at a metalworks in Tunstall. Although Clarice attended the local school where she enjoyed modeling clay pieces, she, like other children of the period, left school at the age of thirteen. Apprenticed as an enameler at Lingard, Webster and Company, she learned freehand painting. After three years, she transferred to Hollingshead and Kirkham where she learned lithography and how to apply transfer prints to pottery. Though not particularly noteworthy in her artistic endeavors, Clarice continued to study at the Tunstall School of Art in the evenings where she furthered her interest in modeling and freehand painting.

Following the onset of World War I, men no longer were available to work in the Staffordshire pottery factories, so women were hired. Clarice acquired a job in Burslem at A. J. Wilkinson in the decorating department. Arthur Shorter had owned the Wilkinson factory since 1896, and eventually was joined by his sons, Guy and Colley. Colley became an important figure in Clarice's life.

As a child, Clarice had spent time with her aunt who worked at Alfred Meakin in the decorating department. Clarice must have enjoyed the visits with her aunt, for she continued to attend art classes, now at the Burslem School of Art. Gordon Forsyth, who later was to become the Superintendent of the Schools of Art in The Potteries area of Staffordshire, taught at the Burslem school. Clarice deemed these lessons important because positions as freehand paintresses at the factories were considered elite and much sought after; Clarice aspired to one of these positions.

By the early 1920s, Clarice noted that she had "progressed as far as modelling clay, keeping patterns in shape books up to date, very fine filigree gilding with a pen, tracing spiders' webs, butterflies etc., to hide small imperfections on expensive ware . . . During this time [she] gained very useful knowledge of making and firing of pottery."[1]

When it came to the making and designing of pottery, Clarice seemed to have an insatiable appetite. Instead of leaving immediately after work like the others, she would wander around the factory examining the various areas and processes. During one of these wanderings, Clarice met Reg Lamb, a young fellow working in the clay area. Reg began to smuggle modeling clay to Clarice. After she had modeled figures, she would then persuade the placers and firemen to fire them for her.

During another of her wanderings, Clarice picked up a piece of pottery and painted a butterfly freehand. The decorating manager at A. J. Wilkinson, Colley's brother-in-law, Jack Walker, noticed it and later showed it to Colley. Feeling that Clarice showed promise, Colley assigned her to work with two of the chief designers, Fred Ridgway and John Butler.[2]

In 1920, Wilkinson's acquired the adjoining Newport Pottery with its warehouse of poor quality pieces. Clarice suggested that the pieces be painted in bold colors to hide the defects; thus *Bizarre* was born. Clarice discovered that triangles were quick to paint and banding could hide the remaining flaws. As Geoffrey Godden, noted author and ceramics expert, observed: "It is noteworthy that at first once unsaleable stock was resurrected and made ultra-modern by the application of basically simple designs that inexpensive semi-skilled labour could master."[3]

In 1922, Howard Carter discovered the tomb of Tutankhamen and inspired a craze for Egyptian motifs in the decorative arts. Perhaps these Egyptian motifs attracted the attention of Clarice as she designed her own version with geometric triangles and exaggerated brush strokes; these were to become an important selling point.

Colley allowed designers their own studios in which to work, moving Clarice to the Newport Pottery where she could work on her modeling. Later, it became obvious that Shorter wanted Clarice away from the Wilkinson's factory for more than just business. Though seventeen years her senior and an upper-class, married man, Colley began to spend much time with Clarice.

In 1927, Colley sent Clarice to the Royal College of Art in London where she studied under the tutelage of Professor Ledward. The professor seemed pleased with Clarice's "natural facility" for modeling. After her two-month course in London, Clarice went to Paris, presumably with Colley, to study the European designs. Clarice must have visited the French museums, for her early geometrical designs in *Bizarre* clearly reflect Cubism and Impressionism. The Fauvists' use of color certainly must have made an impression on Clarice as well. After Clarice's return to England, she bought folios of prints by the French artist Edouard Benedictus entitled *Variations* and *Nouvelle Variations* and two more folios by Serge Gladky.[4]

Colley introduced *Bizarre Ware* at the 1928 British Industries Fair where it gained immediate attention. *Bizarre* designs progressed from simple geometrical patterns to landscapes, but the shapes remained the old Newport and Wilkinson ones. It was around this time that *Crocus* appeared, the design that became Clarice's best-seller. Cleverly designed with flowers hand-painted in downward brush strokes and then inverted for the thin leaves, *Crocus* colors represented, according to Clarice, the "brown earth" and the "yellow sun."

Ethel Barrow, an energetic young paintress, was the first to do the *Crocus* design. Although she worked at Wilkinson's, Clarice had her moved to Newport where she became known as the "*Crocus* girl." Ethel painted the flowers, while Nellie Webb or Winnie Pound added the green brushstrokes that were the leaves. Clara Thomas painted the banding. *Crocus* was Clarice's most popular design, and it was not until 1963 that its sales declined.

The popularity of children's patterns in the late 1920s led Colley Shorter to launch a design created by his eight-year-old daughter, Joan. Each piece was marked with his daughter's name and age. Called *From a child to a child,* the design failed to catch the attention of the buying public, despite the publicity surrounding its release. The idea of marking pieces with a name, however, was one that Colley later used with great success. This name, of course, was Clarice Cliff. The Art Deco Era emphasized limited editions and designer wear, so by the late 1920s many manufacturers created "designer" marks. Pottery manufacturers were no exception. Edward Gray of A. E. Gray & Co. Ltd. had attempted the association of a name with a line of pottery and it was well received. Their backstamp read "Designed by Susie Cooper."

The depressions both in Britain and abroad during the 1930s may have created a market for the brightly colored designs of Clarice Cliff. Although unemployment remained high in the Staffordshire district, the *Bizarre* line kept the Wilkinson and Newport factories in full swing. The "*Bizarre* girls," as Clarice's staff came to be called, even received salary raises.

In a sense, Clarice also received a promotion of her own. On December 21, 1940, she and Colley married. Colley's first wife, Annie, who had been ill for some time, had died the preceding year. Clarice and Colley kept their marriage secret for nearly a year, perhaps because of the class differences or family expectations. As World War II began, government restrictions on pottery manufacturers became a nightmare, so the couple had plenty to keep them busy.

Regulations required manufacturers to export the majority of the products and for goods for the home market to be made with very little decoration. To attract the overseas market, the backstamp was changed to "Royal Staffordshire Ceramics."

An A. J. Wilkinson, Ltd. store display sign promoting Clarice Cliff. *Collection of Carole A. Berk, Ltd*. NP

Clarice's sister, Ethel, married Arthur Steele who had worked at the Wedgwood factory. At Wilkinson's, Steele helped to modernize the equipment by replacing the old bottle kilns with a twin glost kiln and a kiln for firing biscuit. These improvements were important because the Newport factory closed and remained closed after the war.

When the war ended, Colley, now aged 63, returned to work. Clarice, with the help of Hilda Lavatt, her former assistant, began to assemble the "girls" again. Although the Newport factory was no longer in use, Clarice still stamped some pieces with the name for nostalgic reasons.

In 1950, Colley hired Eric Elliot from the Burslem School of Art as an assistant art director. He reissued some of Clarice's earlier designs. At this time, tableware made for export to North America could be covered in decoration, which appealed to Clarice, though English wares were still not allowed to be decorated all over, a prohibition that continued until 1952. The designs of *Ophelia,* which has just begun production before the war, and *Chelsea Basket* must have appealed to the American market. *Crocus* appeared in more subtle colors, which can also be said for *My Garden*. The latter used matt glazes and a greater variety of shapes. Another pattern exported to America was the *Georgian*, with its gold and turquoise or gold and green edge lining.

By the mid-1950s, Clarice and Colley spent less and less time at the factory due to their failing health. To make matters worse, in 1954, Eric Elliot resigned. The new modern designs aroused consumers' interests, but without a contemporary designer, Wilkinson's sales declined. With the loss of the market share abroad and the negative effects of a new sales tax on domestic sales, the factory's former glory ended. Adding to the difficulties Clarice faced, Colley died in 1963.

Clarice's health prevented her from rejuvenating the factory and in 1964 she sold the firm to a competitor, Midwinter. On October 23, 1972, Clarice died at the age of seventy-three.[5]

The Designs

The designs of Clarice Cliff fall into ranges. Sometimes these ranges overlapped as new glazes came into production. The first and perhaps most well-known range is *Bizarre*, which dates from 1928 to 1936. From 1930 to 1931, Clarice introduced her colorful *Appliqué* designs which used expensive enamels outlined in Indian ink. The year of 1929 saw the production of *Fantasque* with its hand-painted designs. This production continued until 1934, a particularly busy period for Clarice Cliff. Many *Fantasque* pieces were mistakenly marked *Bizarre* during this time.

Also in 1929, *Inspiration* and *Latona* appeared. These ranges employed glaze as the primary decoration. The metallic oxide glazes in purple, brown, pink, or blue covered the *Inspiration* pieces which were fired at a higher temperature than *Bizarre*. *Latona* wares displayed a whitish glaze with designs done in freehand. The production of *Inspiration* ended in 1930, while *Latona* production lasted two more years. Clarice's designs were often inspired by artistic styles and not specifics; therefore, her designs do not fall neatly into classifications such as Art

Deco. Instead, she combined the Art Deco with Art Nouveau, Cubism, Fauvism, and other trends to create designs uniquely her own.

The Shapes

Prior to 1929, Clarice decorated old Newport shapes because new shapes were expensive to produce. In 1919, Newport had begun numbering its shapes to simplify ordering. By 1928, the numbers reached 342. In 1929, Clarice began designing new shapes, so the numbers after 342 reflect her influence. Shapes 358 through 360 were designed to make the pieces easier to paint.

Clarice felt the old shapes "out of step" with her ideas, so she created the sleek *Dover* shape which remained popular until the mid-30s. Other original shapes included the *Yo-Yo* vase, the *Daffodil* shapes, and the *Castellated* vase, just to name a few.

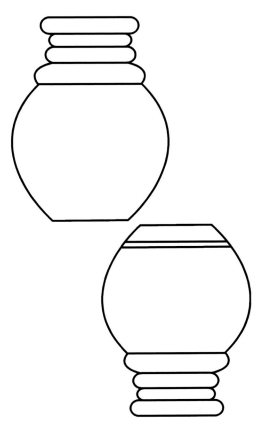

Shape 358 became . . . shape 362.

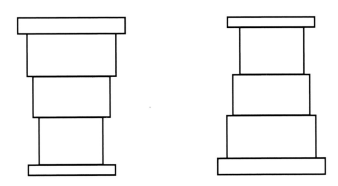

Shape 369 became. . . shape 392.

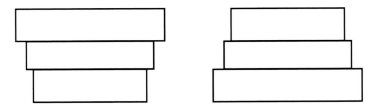

Shape 368 turned into . . . 391.

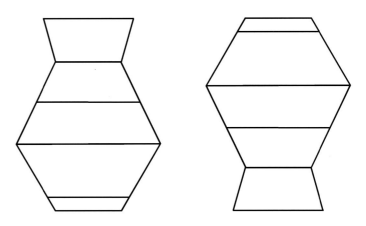

Shape 360 when inverted appeared . . . as shape 365.

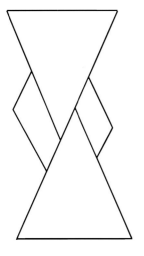

Yo-Yo Vase

Daffodil Coffee Pot

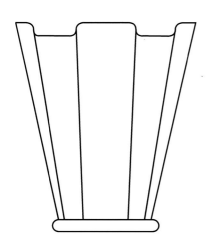

Castellated Vase

Clarice inverted old shapes to make new ones. The large-top tiered or "stepped" vase, shapes 368 and 369, became the candleholder shapes of 391 and 392. The most noteworthy inversions are shapes 358 to 362 and 360 to 365. One of the most popular Clarice Cliff pieces is the *Lotus* jug. In 1919, this jug had been designed as part of a toilet set. Clarice began using it as a decorative jug, so the shape name was changed to *Isis.* Collectors, however, seem to prefer the name *Lotus* and save *Isis* for the jugs with no handles.

Early in 1929, the tiered vases must have been influenced by Robert Lallemant, a designer whose work Clarice saw in *Mobilier et Décoration* magazine. Clarice also copied shape 370 from a globe design in *Mobilier et Décoration*. Also in 1929, a 1% iron oxide gave a honey color to the glaze without giving it the heavy look that the 2% oxides had done. These lighter glazes seemed appropriate for Clarice's designs.[6]

The factory usually held two copies of the design books, one for the factory or the "dirty copy" and another for the library. When viewing the *A. J. Wilkinson and Newport Pottery Collection Pattern Book Containing Miscellaneous Designs c. 192-195-*, now held in the archives at the Hanley Library in Stoke-on-Trent, one sees sketches of designs are colored in watercolors, some with names like "Tropical Fruit and Spice" and "Breadfruit." Occasionally, one reads significant comments regarding the designs or shapes, presumably in Clarice's own handwriting. For instance, notes such as "I don't like it which means that it will probably be the best seller. Can you sketch it up in turquoise and grey and pink and grey" (30) appear as well as other notes like "I hate modern, but I think this will sell."

Clarice remarks that the barware with barbershop quartet faces represents an "excellent idea for some sort of 'fancy.' The question is what? Other than plates, which we don't want, round mugs? larger bar ashtray, pretzel or chip bowl" (75). As an administrator, Clarice deftly remarked: "don't like this. too heavy, as women buyers say 'it doesn't *do* anything to me'" (114).

In the "buying office" pattern book of *Shapes and Designs by Clarice Cliff*, notes regarding a "Blackbird Pie Funnel Modelled by Clarice Cliff" read: "this rather amusing little pie funnel has proved enormously interesting to the public, for since it was on the market we have been inundated with demands—It retails at the ridiculous price of 6d [shillings], so they can be used not only as pie funnels, but table decorations for parties" (54). Designed in 1933, these "pie birds," as they came to be called, were reproduced after the patent ran out.

The pattern book that contains *Rules of Bizarre Ware, Views of the Factories and Clarice Cliff at Work c.192-195-* dictates that the *Secrets* design should be "finished in soft toning shades of green, yellow & brown" and that the "flower basket or fruit" pattern should be "finished in velvety matt glazes 3 colors, mushroom, verdant green & cream."

In the *A. J. Wilkinson's and Newport Pottery Collection: Advertising and Price Lists for English and Overseas Pottery (c. 195-)*, there are photos not only of Clarice Cliff herself, but also photos of her wares used for advertising purposes. Moreover, notes by her with descriptions also appear. She writes of *Rodanthe:* a "Modern Flower Vase No. 674/3" that it is "a warm honeyglaze background done in beautiful toning [the addition of grey to the base color] shades of orange Fawn Yellow & Grey. Another style of colouring Blue Green Fawn & Pink and can also be obtained in Green Pink Fawn Grey & Yellow" for the "Retail Price 12/0 each."

Clarice Cliff also made comments regarding designs such as *Goldstone* and *Eton. Goldstone*, though not commercially viable at the time, was perhaps one of Clarice's most creative designs; it carries these remarks: " . . . the effect being produced by actually including bits of metal in the mixing of the body. Finished in a number of different styles in bright toning colors. Retail prices: flower jug 10/. Figure 25/" (115). Of the flower vase decorated in *Hydrangea*, Clarice writes: "The floral part is done in soft colours, toning greens, toning oranges and yellows. This vase, being only a few inches from bak [*sic*] to front is particularly suitable for use on the new narrow fireplaces and surrounds" (112).

Forgeries

Since the rise in popularity of designs by Clarice Cliff, forgeries such as the *Orange Roof Cottage Lotus* jug have surfaced. The forgery has reflections in the windows of the cottage and the bridge has incorrect proportions. Furthermore, the orange banding is too red and too bright. The older colors contained toxins, so they are no longer available. The forgeries frequently include a backstamp; however, the original Clarice Cliff backstamp was added by means of a rubber stamp with black ink or a lithograph overglaze. Normally, *Bizarre* was included with the mark.[7]

Other forgeries that have surfaced include the sugar shaker in *Orange Erin, Sungay, Red Roofs*, and *House & Bridge*. As in the case of the *Lotus* jug, the colors are too bright. The best advice for beginning collectors is to become familiar with the authentic pieces, either by visiting reputable dealers or noteworthy auction houses. The old adage "knowledge is power" certainly holds true for collectors. It is less likely that collectors will fall prey to unscrupulous or uninformed sellers, if they view and handle verifiable pieces.

Weight is often a telltale sign. Since most reproductions cannot duplicate the item *exactly,* either due to legal restrictions or an inability to obtain original clays, paints, and molds, I have found that handling the objects often indicates much more than is visible to the eye. If the piece doesn't feel right, it probably isn't! Better to pass on it and look elsewhere. Of course, even the most informed collector is not infallible; frequently there are no guarantees, so buyer beware! Buying from reputable dealers is the safest way to add to any collection. Reputable dealers guarantee their merchandise and educate their customers about it.

Pitchers and Jugs

Clarice Cliff created pitchers in a range of unusual shapes, from the rather classical lines of the *Athens* shape to the curved lines and small ball feet of the *Bon Jour* shape. The angled lines of the *Conical* shape offered a strikingly original creation for the consumer.

The *Lotus* shape originally appeared as part of a set, but Clarice redesigned it. Perhaps one of the most popular pieces, it is also one of the most expensive shapes.

Price range for pitchers: $600 to $3,000 and up. *Lotus* and *Isis* Jugs range from $3,000 and up. Unless otherwise indicated, prices are per piece.

Newlyn, a design produced from 1935-1937, is shown here on a 6.75-inch pitcher. *Collection of Carole A. Berk, Ltd*. Medium

1930 witnessed the appearance of the net design known as *Tennis,* a pattern similar to *Football* but without any black. Production ceased in 1931. Shown here on a 6.25-inch pitcher with the *Athens* shape. *Courtesy of CARA Antiques.* High

A 1933 *Bizarre* pattern entitled *Rudyard*, ceased production in 1934. *Collection of Carole A. Berk, Ltd.* Medium

The *Athens* shape also complements this *Latona* pattern called *Zap. Courtesy of CARA Antiques.* Rare

Aptly named, this 1930 pattern called *Picasso Flower* certainly is reminiscent of the artist and his Cubist paintings. Shown here in red on an 8″ pitcher. The pattern also appears in orange and in blue. *Courtesy of CARA Antiques*. Hard To Find

The *Alton* design on a *Daffodil* shape 8-inch pitcher. Note the handle. *Courtesy of CARA Antiques*. Medium

These two *Fantasque* pitchers are shape 36 and are 6.25" high: *Autumn* (1930-1934) and *Berries* (1930-1932). Both have the *Cafe-au-Lait* stippled ground. *Collection of Carole A. Berk, Ltd.* Medium

A *Green Apples* design on a Crown shape pitcher. *Collection of Carole A. Berk, Ltd.* Low

The landscape on these *Sunray* (*Night & Day*) pitchers reflects a Cubist influence. Created in 1929, this pattern was discontinued in 1930. *Collection of Carole A. Berk, Ltd.* High+

The blue fruit and large orange bands contrast nicely with the simple lines of this pitcher. *Collection of Carole A. Berk, Ltd.* Low to Medium

Designed in 1933, *Goldstone* never seemed to catch the attention of the consuming public. Rather plain in contrast to the other designs of the period and difficult to manufacture, it was nonetheless quite creative. Production ceased after one year. Shown here on a 6.5-inch bulbous jug. *Collection of Carole A. Berk, Ltd.* Low

These bright flowers of the *Nasturtium* (1932-1934) design border a *Cafe-au-Lait* ground. This pitcher is 9.5" in height. *Courtesy of CARA Antiques.* Low to Medium

Rather unlike other Clarice Cliff pieces, this pitcher has runnings, places where the glaze has been allowed to run or drip, as a part of the decoration. The unusual purple handle sharply contrasts with the tan body on this *My Garden* piece. The pattern originated in 1934 and continued until 1941. After the war, production resumed. *Collection of Carole A. Berk, Ltd.* Low

"Seven Colors" for this *Secrets* 10-inch *Lotus* jug is quite unusual for the pattern. *Collection of Carole A. Berk, Ltd.* Hard to Find

A close-up showing the details of the pattern. Note the upward movement of the design and the solitary black, vertical line. *Collection of Carole A. Berk, Ltd.*

These two early geometric designs (right and opposite page) exemplify the bright colors that give Clarice Cliff ceramics much of its appeal. Note the brushstrokes in the detail of the pattern. Cliff felt that consumers wanted hand-painted pieces, so she exaggerated the strokes. *Collection of Carole A. Berk, Ltd.* High+

Unlike many of the early Cliff geometric designs with their bright oranges and reds, this double-handled geometric *Lotus* jug displays a deep purple coupled with green. Notice the exaggerated strokes on this jug as well. *Collection of Carole A. Berk, Ltd.* Hard to Find

Black nicely complements the bright orange of this *Fantasque Lotus* jug. *Collection of Carole A. Berk, Ltd*. High+

Pastel colors give this *Alpine* scene a fresh feeling. The vertical planes contrasting the horizontal bands add a sense of movement toward the warmth of the cottage. *Courtesy of CARA Antiques.* High+

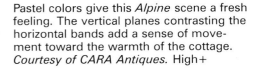

This *Lotus* jug of *Latona Bouquet* with its bright, circular bursts of red and yellow against the vertical and diagonal movement of the background clearly exemplifies the artistic and creative abilities of Clarice Cliff. *Courtesy of CARA Antiques*. High+

The young paintresses under Clarice Cliff's direction painted the *Crocus* pattern by decorating the flowers with downward brushstrokes. They then inverted the piece and with similar strokes painted the leaves. This very clever design became one of Cliff's most successful patterns. Shown here on an *Isis* jug. *Collection of Carole A. Berk, Ltd.* High+

The mark on the *Isis* jug includes not only the *Bizarre* by Clarice Cliff mark, but also the name of the design and the name of the shape. *Isis* indicates the *Lotus* jug shape without handles. *Collection of Carole A. Berk, Ltd.*

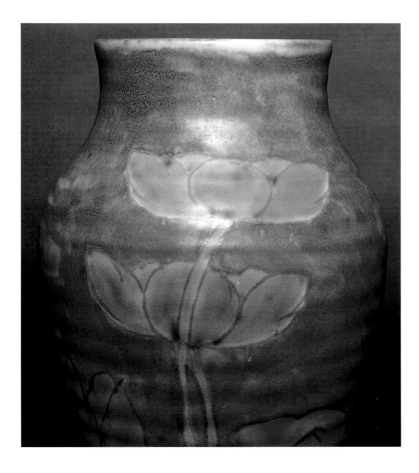

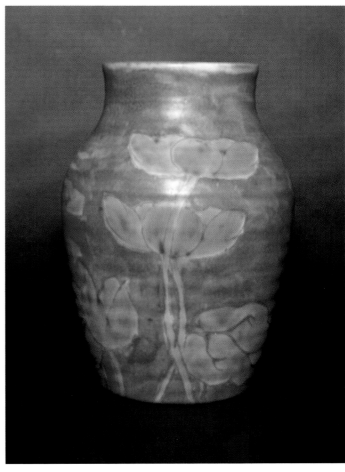

On this *Inspiration* (1929-1930) *Isis* jug, we again see a variation of the purple-green combination used on the earlier geometric jug. *Collection of Carole A. Berk, Ltd.* High+

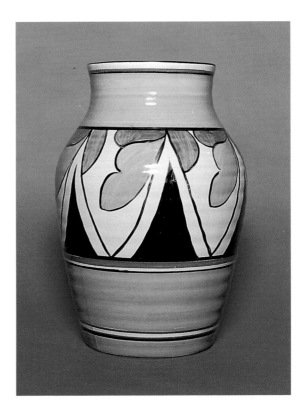

This early geometric piece uses the orange and black combination seen in many Clarice Cliff designs. *Collection of Carole A. Berk, Ltd.* High+

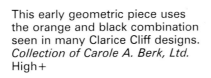

This *Isis* jug in the *Latona* range utilizes the *Stained Glass* design most efficiently. *Collection of Carole A. Berk, Ltd.* High+

Teaware and Coffee Services

Clarice Cliff designed tea sets in many of her most popular shapes. An Early Morning Set includes a service for two: the teapot, cream pitcher, sugar bowl, and two cups with saucers and a serving plate. The teapot, cream pitcher, and sugar bowl are referred to as a "Trio." Coffee Services generally included a service for six or eight. Teaware and Coffee Services appeared on the market in nearly a dozen shapes, in addition to several novelty designs.

This category has perhaps one of the most variable price ranges because of the variety of shapes and designs. Because so much depends on the combination, it is difficult to indicate prices. However, as a guideline, the lower end of the range runs around $250 to $800 with the mid-range averaging up to about $1,500. The high end may start around $1,500, but extends well beyond that price depending on how many pieces in the set, how rare the pattern, or some of the other factors previously mentioned. Since much teaware and often coffee services are sold in trios or sets, sometimes the price indicated represents more than one piece; this is noted in the caption.

An *Autumn Crocus* teapot with underplate. The paintresses painted the flowers with limited brushstrokes. *Collection of Carole A. Berk, Ltd.* Low

An *Original Bizarre* teapot and a sugar bowl. Both have early geometric designs. *Collection of Carole A. Berk, Ltd.* Hard to Find

A tea set in the *Bon Jour* shape. The *Viscaria* teapot and sugar bowl are accompanied by an *Aurea* creamer. *Collection of Carole A. Berk, Ltd.* Medium

A floral teapot in the *Bon Jour* shape with tea cup. *Collection of Carole A. Berk, Ltd.* Medium

A *Bizarre* tea set, or Trio as the three pieces are sometimes called, in the 1933 *Cowslip* design on a green *Cafe-au-Lait* ground. *Collection of Carole A. Berk, Ltd.* High+ for set

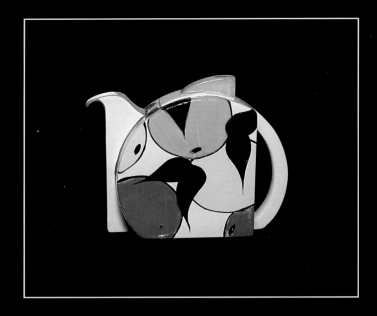

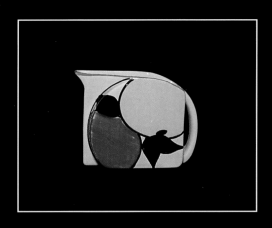

This Stamford shape *Oranges and Apples* teapot and matching creamer are marked both *Fantasque* and *Bizarre.* During 1929 and the early 1930s, an extremely busy period, many pieces were marked with both names. *Courtesy of CARA Antiques.* High

Marked *Bizarre* and *Fantasque*, this *Conical* teapot measures 5.5" and has a *House and Bridge* design, c.1931-1933. *Courtesy of CARA Antiques.* Medium

This *Latona Stained Glass Conical* teapot (1929-1930) marked *Bizarre* is 5.5" in height. *Courtesy of CARA Antiques.* Medium

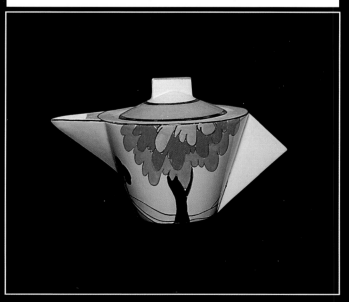

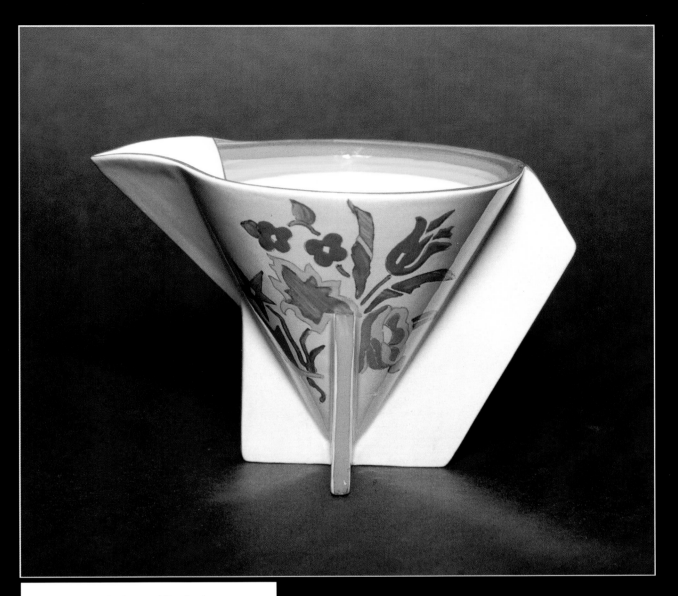

This *Woman's Journal Conical* creamer, presented as a mail order item by the *Woman's Journal* magazine, dates from 1931. *Collection of Carole A. Berk, Ltd.* Low

The other side of the creamer has the Clarice Cliff signature near the handle. Shown here with a small plate of the same design. *Collection of Carole A. Berk, Ltd.*

These *Woman's Journal* cups feature the *Bizarre by Clarice Cliff* mark. *Courtesy of Carole A. Berk, Ltd*. Low

Left and above:
A *Bizarre* cup and saucer in the appropriately named *Gay Day* (1930-1934) design. Note the pattern name above the mark. A similar pattern was produced with yellow, blue, and green asters and was called *Sun Gay*. *Collection of Carole A. Berk, Ltd*. Low

A *Gibraltar* (1931-1932) coffee service for six which includes serving pieces along with plates, cups, and saucers. *May Avenue, Antiquarius, London*. NP

Shown here is an *Original Bizarre* coffee pot in an early geometric design with pieces from the set: a creamer and sugar bowl as well as a cup with saucer. Before Clarice Cliff began designing her own shapes, she used old Newport shapes and painted them in brightly colored triangles. Pay close attention to the over-exaggerated brushstrokes. *Collection of Carole A. Berk, Ltd.* NP

This *Idyll*, also known as *Crinoline Lady* (1931-1936), design complements the *Conical* shape of the coffee pot. Vertical lines with a strong red base anchor the piece while the lighter pastels draw the eye upward. *Courtesy of CARA Antiques.* Medium

A *Yoo Hoo* conical coffee pot has a striking red handle contrasting the black body, c.1930-1931. *Collection of Carole A. Berk, Ltd.* Medium

These pieces are part of a *Capri* coffee set. This design originated in 1933, but was discontinued in 1934. *Collection of Carole A. Berk, Ltd.* Low

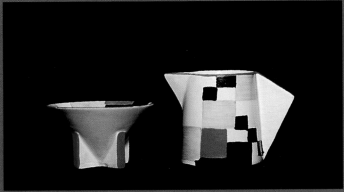

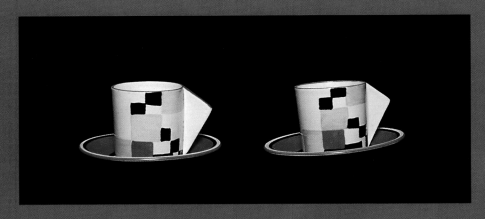

Plates

Clarice Cliff's originality extended even to such simple items as plates. Plates make a wonderful collection, since their simple shapes beautifully display the design. The hexagonal plates offered ideal surfaces for the geometric designs, while the *Biarritz* shape complemented the simpler designs.

The price range for this category averages between $225 and $600, unless otherwise noted.

The *Crocus* pattern also appeared on plates. Observe the spiraling pattern of the brown center, probably done with a single brushstroke while the plate turned on a potter's wheel. *Collection of Carole A. Berk, Ltd.* Medium

This *Delecia Citrus* 6-inch plate, with the telltale glaze runnings in the design, carries the name of the pattern along with the *Bizarre* mark on the back. In addition to plain *Delecia*, other patterns in the series include *Pansies, Daisy,* and *Poppy,* which means that these flowers replaced the citrus fruit at the top edge of the design. Created by mixing turpentine with the color before application, these colors varied from an orange/green combination to one of pastels. *Collection of Carole A. Berk, Ltd.* Medium

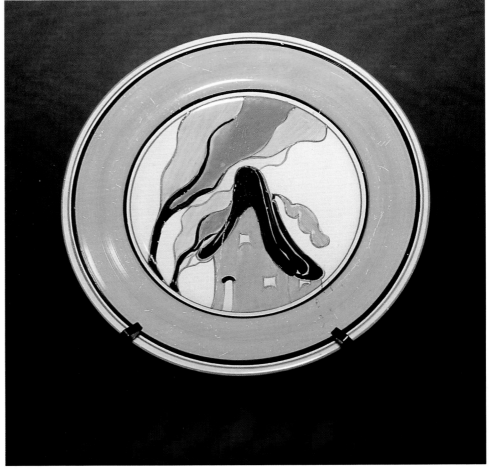

Like the cottage in the *Alpine* pattern, this *Orange House* has an inviting appearance with smoke rising from its chimney—a protection against the chill of the strong wind outside. Called simply *Orange House,* this *Fantasque* pattern was produced from 1930-1932. *Collection of Carole A. Berk, Ltd.* High+

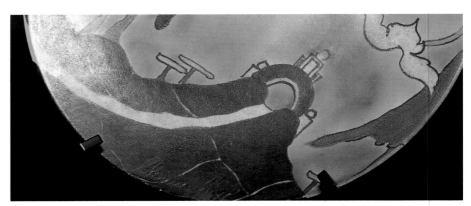

Left and below:
This *Inspiration Caprice* has a
Clarice Cliff signature at the
bottom. Collection of *Carole A.
Berk, Ltd.* Rare

A rare pattern, this 10-inch
plate depicts the 1929
Persian (Original) design.
*Collection of Carole A.
Berk, Ltd.* Rare

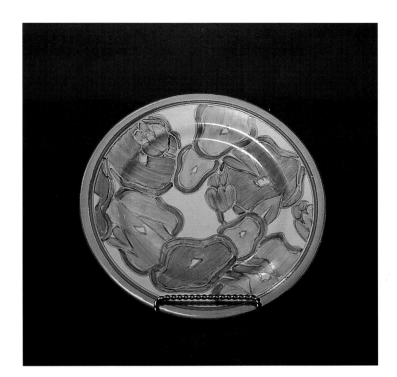

Quite unlike other productions that used the same pattern name, Clarice Cliff's *Chintz* uses large buds and leaves in the design. Here shown in blue, the pattern also appeared in orange. *Collection of Carole A. Berk, Ltd.* High

The small cottage appears dwarfed by the large trees on this *Biarritz* plate. *Collection of Carole A. Berk, Ltd.* High

Rhodanthe first appeared in 1934 and continued in production until the war. *Collection of Carole A. Berk, Ltd.* Low

This geometric pattern on this 6-inch plate complements its hexagonal shape. *Collection of Carole A. Berk, Ltd.* Medium

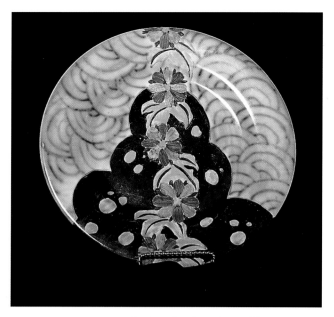

An *Inspiration* plate with delightful color combinations. *Collection of Carole A. Berk, Ltd*. NP

The shape of this *Biarritz* plate nicely encircles the figure in *Idyll. Collection of Carole A. Berk, Ltd.* High

Observe the brushstrokes on these *Gay Day* flowers. *Collection of Carole A. Berk, Ltd.* Low

Two plates with center designs encircled by orange. The bold combination of the triangular designs surrounded by a wide, bright orange border cleverly combines bold patterns for interest. The more delicate flowers and small orange band on the *Woman's Journal* pattern seem quite sedate by comparison. *Collection of Carole A. Berk, Ltd.* Low

Forest Glen, a 1935-1937 *Bizarre* design, utilizes the runnings similar to the *Delecia* patterns. The carefully balanced upward and downward movement in the design is anchored by the cottage as a focal point. Unlike other pieces decorated with the same design, the plate clearly displays the clever balance of the pattern. *Collection of Carole A. Berk, Ltd.* High

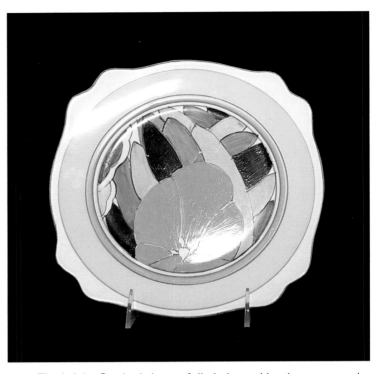

The bright *Gardenia* is carefully balanced by the green and black leaves and a yellow border. *Courtesy of CARA Antiques.* High

This 9-inch plate, like many other Cliff designs, has a cottage to anchor the design. Here, the design is *Orange Roof Cottage. Courtesy of Witney & Airault (Decorative Arts).* Medium

Yet another plate with an orange border. This early abstract focuses on the stylized triangles of the sails in the *Bizarre* range *Harbour Scene* or *Xanthic* from 1932-1933. *Collection of Carole A. Berk, Ltd.* High

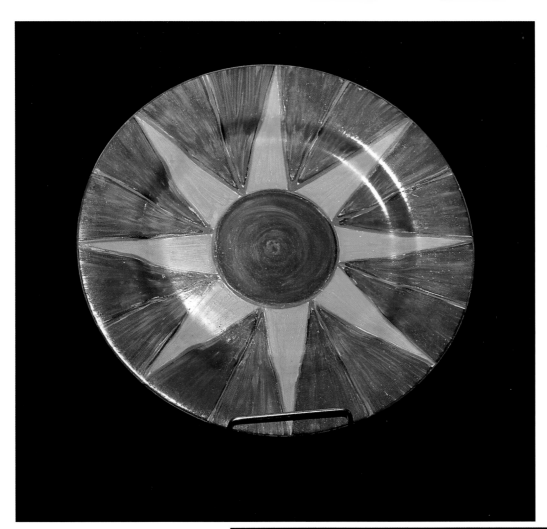

The orange starburst with a cobalt focal point is an early geometric design. *Collection of Carole A. Berk, Ltd.* Medium

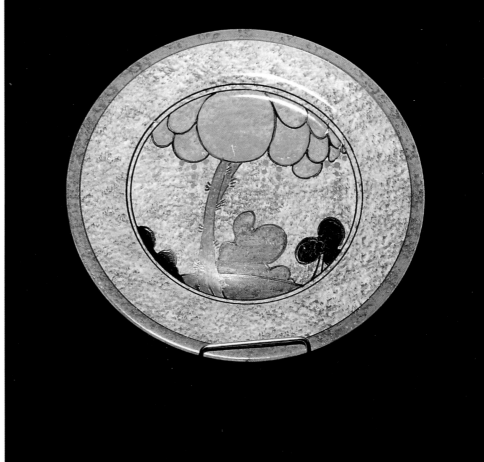

A *Cafe-au-Lait* pattern, this design was one of several that appeared from 1931-1934. *Collection of Carole A. Berk, Ltd*. Medium

Dame Laura Knight decorated a series of "Circus" plates, usually painted in pink. Here, the example is painted in blue on a white body and is part of a set of six. The name on the back, *Willow,* likens the design to the tableware of the same name. *Collection of Carole A. Berk, Ltd.* NP

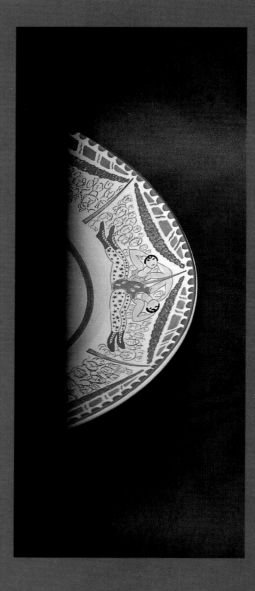

Naked ladies decorate this plate by Dame Laura Knight. *Collection of Carole A. Berk, Ltd.* NP

Bowls and Lidded Jars

Tiered bowls, bowls in the *Daffodil* or *Conical* shape, and hexagonal bowls are just a few of the wonderfully creative examples provided by Clarice Cliff. The bowls vary in price according to shape, size, and design, along with collectibility. In the 1920s, with the oriental influence still strong, ginger jars became popular. Oriental imports, along with those from Persia, perhaps inspired such designs as *Inspiration*. This design certainly seems appropriate for a ginger jar.

The price for bowls starts around $400 to $900 for the lower end of the scale. The midrange pieces average between $975 to $1,500 and the high end of the category begins around $1,600 and continues upward. Lidded jars average similar prices, but on the higher end of each of the ranges.

If pattern could be said to indicate function, this 8.5-inch *Fantasque Melon* or *Picasso Fruit* bowl is an appropriately titled design. *Collection of Carole A. Berk, Ltd.* Very Rare (especially in red and blue)

Although this *Football* pattern closely resembles *Tennis*, *Football* has black in the design. *Collection of Carole A. Berk, Ltd.* High

This *Fantasque* 3" x 4.25" hexago-
nal bowl is decorated with the
Gibraltar pattern. *Collection of
Carole A. Berk, Ltd.* Medium

This daffodil shaped bowl is 12.5" x
6.75" and is the *Bridgewater* design,
c.1934. *Courtesy of CARA Antiques.*
High

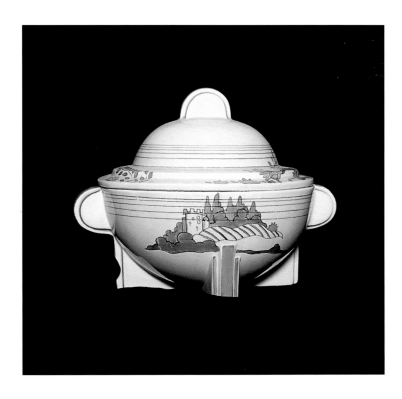

A castle scene decorates this lidded bowl. *Collection of Carole A. Berk, Ltd*. High

The *Inspiration Caprice* on this large ginger jar causes the eye to move around the jar with the diagonal movement of the design. *Collection of Carole A. Berk, Ltd.* NP

Lidded tureens and a pitcher in the *Biarritz* shape, c.1932. *Courtesy of Witney & Airault (Decorative Arts).* NP

An unusual piece, this ginger jar has the *Sliced Fruit* design. The lid repeats the circular patterns in the fruit, but in a solid color. *Collection of Carole A. Berk, Ltd.* High to High+

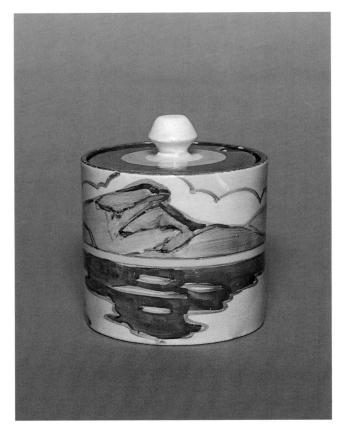

These two 4-inch *Fantasque* jam pots represent opposite sides of the world: *Gibraltar* and *Honolulu*. *Collection of Carole A. Berk, Ltd.* Medium

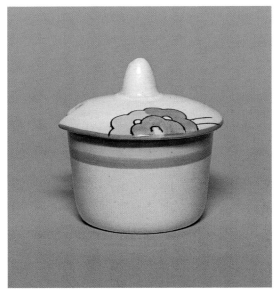

This *Nemesia* mustard jar stands 2" tall. *Collection of Carole A. Berk, Ltd.* Low

This mustard jar displays an *Original Bizarre* geometric pattern. *Courtesy of CARA Antiques.* Low

Two honey jars with bees perched on the top: a *Fantasque* pattern and a *Japan* pattern. *Collection of Carole A. Berk, Ltd.* Low to Medium

Windbells is displayed here on a biscuit jar. *Courtesy of CARA Antiques.* Medium

This *Crocus* 5.5-inch biscuit jar is complemented by a bright yellow lid. All shades of yellow were popular on ceramics during the Art Deco period. *Collection of Carole A. Berk, Ltd.* Medium

To contrast the static appearance of the slim, horizontal bands, the flowering *Hydrangea* design running diagonally across the bands creates a forceful, yet flowing movement. *Collection of Carole A. Berk, Ltd.* Low

A *Fantasque* biscuit jar with a bright orange flower. Unlike many Cliff floral designs, which are painted fully open, this flower is viewed from the side. *Collection of Carole A. Berk, Ltd.* Medium

This oriental-looking house is part of a *Firs* design. *Collection of Carole A. Berk, Ltd.* Medium

Vases

Wilkinson's and Newport Pottery offered vases in a wide variety of styles, from tiered to castellated. As in the case with other Clarice Cliff examples, prices vary according to the design/shape combination, as well as other factors. Sometimes, due to the rarity of the design on a particular shape, the smallest pieces bring the highest prices.

The price range for the vases begins around a few hundred dollars and extends to around $700. The mid-range is around $2,000 with the higher ranges averaging $3,500 and up.

This *Circle Tree* (also known as *RAF Tree*) was created in 1929. Clarice Cliff copied the globe shape, numbered 370, from *Mobilier et Décoration*. *Collection of Carole A. Berk, Ltd.* High

A number of Clarice Cliff's designs in the early 1930s used stylized trees. This *Patina Tree* (1932-1933) resembles other tree patterns, but is somewhat unique in its coloring. *Collection of Carole A. Berk, Ltd.* High

A *Honolulu* pattern made between 1933 and 1935. *Collection of Carole A. Berk, Ltd.* Medium

This *Latona Bouquet* globe vase is
artistically very well-conceived.
Collection of Carole A. Berk, Ltd.
High

Oranges, a *Bizarre* pattern created
in 1931, ceased production in
1932. *Collection of Carole A. Berk,
Ltd.* Medium

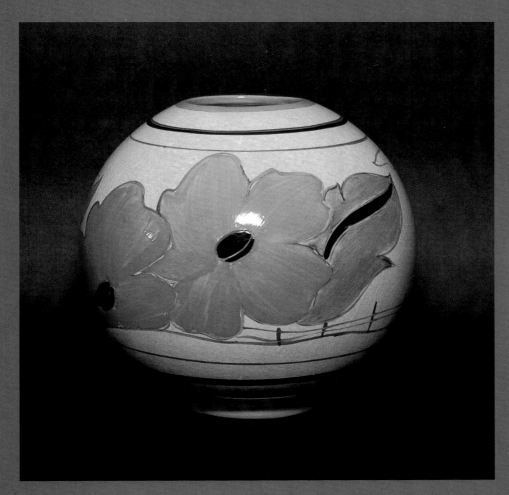

Two *Cafe-au-Lait* patterned globes: one in floral motif and the other in *Trees & House*. *Collection of Carole A. Berk, Ltd.* Medium

Marked *Fantasque* and *Bizarre*,
this *Summerhouse* (1931-1933)
vase is 8.25" high. *Courtesy of
CARA Antiques.* Medium

Shown here is an 8.25-inch
Fantasque vase in shape 358 using
typical Cliff colors: orange, cobalt,
and green. *Collection of Carole A.
Berk, Ltd.* Medium

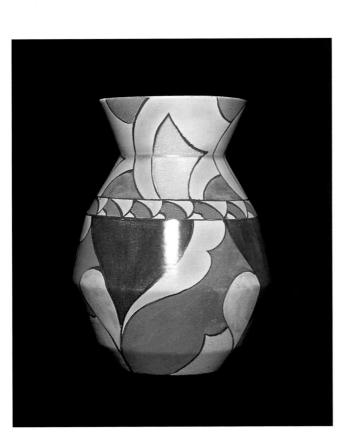

The varying shades of *Inspiration*
blues on this shape 360 vase
contrast with the lighter pinks of
the design. *Collection of Carole A.
Berk, Ltd.* Medium

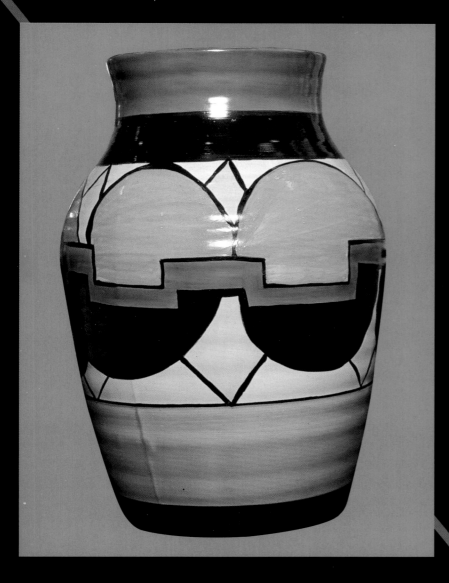

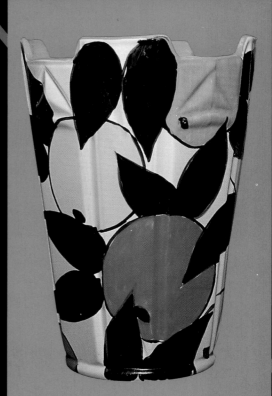

These two jugs have a "castellated" design: the 10-inch *Isis* jug has a castellated line through the center of the circles, while the *Oranges and Lemons* vase (shape 451) has a castellated top edge. *Courtesy of CARA Antiques*. High

On these 6.25-inch *Sungold* vases, variations occur because they are hand-painted by different paintresses. Note the differences in color and size of the pattern between the two vases. *Collection of Carole A. Berk, Ltd.* Low

An 8-inch *Crocus* vase in an easily recognized shape, number 269. *Collection of Carole A. Berk, Ltd.* Low

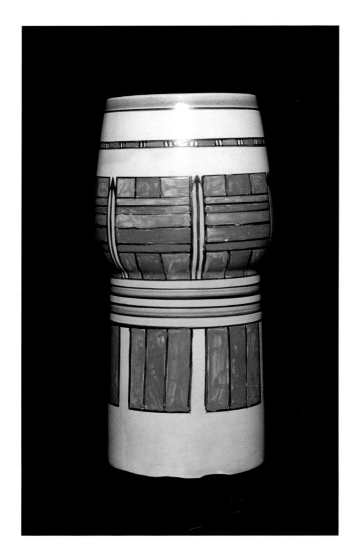

Right:
A similar shaped vase with an *Inspiration* pattern, 6.26" in height. *Courtesy of CARA Antiques.* Rare

Left:
Horizontal bands complement the vertical lines of this vase as well as the pattern on the vase itself. *Collection of Carole A. Berk, Ltd.* Low

This shape seems ideal for the *Alton* design. Vase is 8" in height. *Courtesy of CARA Antiques*. Medium to High

The tall, triangular *Summerhouse* is balanced by circular trees flanking it on each side. As in other designs, Cliff made use of a red base to anchor the design and a yellow top rim to draw the eye upward. *Courtesy of CARA Antiques*. High

A typical Cliff shaped 6.5-inch vase displays an early geometric design. *Collection of Carole A. Berk, Ltd.* Medium

The vertical lines of the shape contrast with the wavy lines of the *Sunrise* design to draw the eye upward and around. Cliff's designs are filled with movement even in the seemingly simple pieces. *Courtesy of CARA Antiques.* High

The deceptively simple, brown *Dolphin* 8-inch vase still depicts motion with the arching of the fish against the waves. *Collection of Carole A. Berk, Ltd.* Low

These two 4.5-inch vases decorated in opposite ways look totally different. The primary and secondary colors used by Cliff with such pizzazz brighten the *Bobbins* vase, while the more sedate colors and wavy, concentric circles subdue the *Goldstone* one. *Collection of Carole A. Berk, Ltd*. Medium and Low respectively

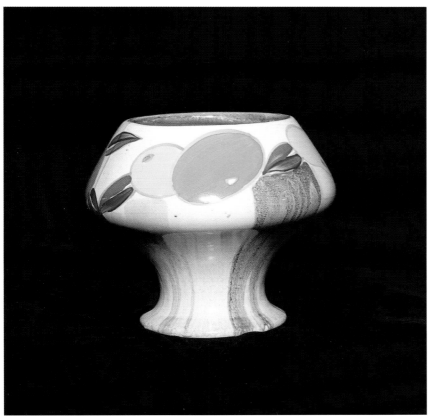

A 2.25-inch vase displays the *Crocus* design. *Collection of Carole A. Berk, Ltd*. Low

The *Delecia Citrus* design perfectly parallels the shape of this vase. *Collection of Carole A. Berk, Ltd.* Medium

The flowers on the handle of *My Garden* aptly accent the curves on the fan pattern of the *Inspiration* glaze. Inside the vase is a frog for holding flower stems. *Collection of Carole A. Berk, Ltd.* High

The shape of this tiered vase, shown here with *Delecia* and *Forest Glen*, became the shape of a candleholder when inverted, a testament to the creativity of Clarice Cliff. *Collection of Carole A. Berk, Ltd.* Low to Medium

An *Inspiration Rose* design on a *Yo-Yo* vase. *May Avenue, Antiquarius, London.* Very Rare

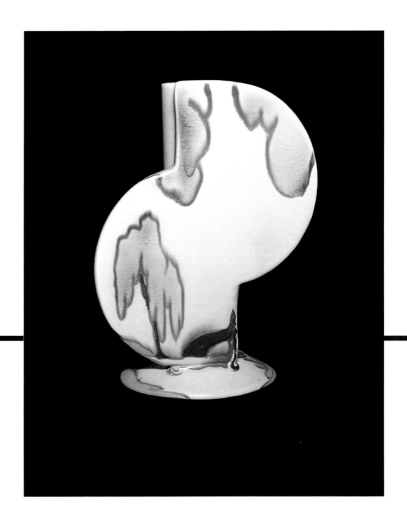

Right and far right:
The slender trunk and the ballooning branches of the tree's design correlate with the shape of this finned Stamford vase. *Collection of Carole A. Berk, Ltd.* High

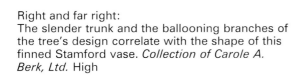

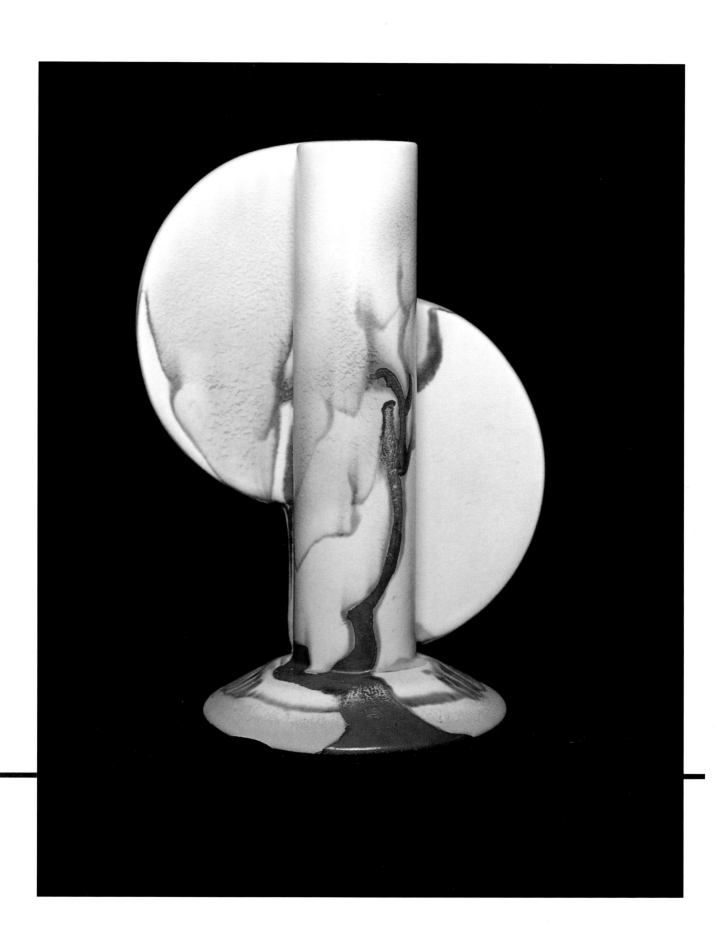

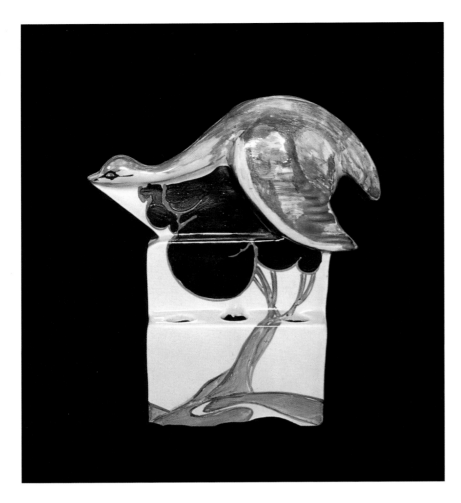

Art Deco consumers must have enjoyed the creativity of this swan flower-block, shape 423. *Collection of Carole a. Berk, Ltd.* Rare

Forest Glen is seen here on a daffodil shaped vase (shape 450). *Collection of Carole A. Berk, Ltd.* Medium

These daffodil vases were suitable for a variety of designs. The two shown here are *Green Erin* (1933-1934) and *Blue Firs* (1933-1937). *Courtesy of CARA Antiques.* Medium

Ashtrays

During the Art Deco years, both men and women smoked. A sign of sophistication, smoking utensils provided manufacturers with an entire range of necessary paraphernalia. Everything from cigarette cases to ashtrays became fashionable. Note the variety of ashtrays presented in Clarice Cliff designs.

The prices for the ashtrays average between $200 to $500.

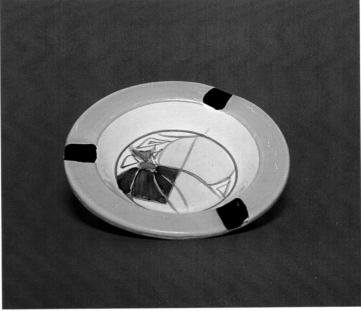

Left, above, and following 5 pages:
Smoking among both sexes gained momentum in the 1920s. Considered common courtesy to offer cigarettes from a cigarette case, smokers even offered ones to persons known not to smoke. Consequently, the Art Deco era abounded with smoking utensils, especially ashtrays. The variety of designs presented on ashtrays is indicative of their popularity. All photos from the *Collection of Carole A. Berk, Ltd.* (See text for price range)

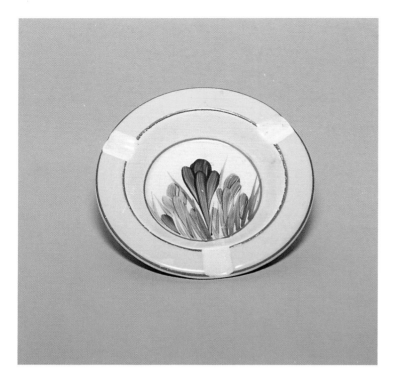

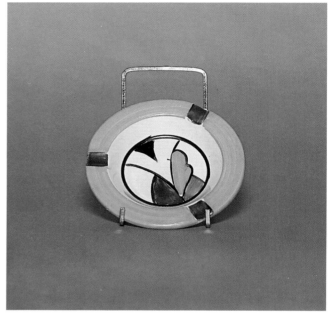

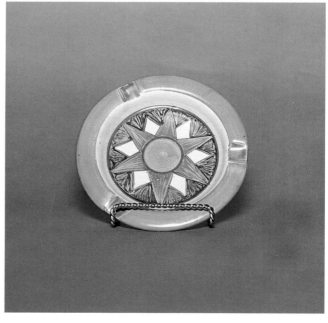

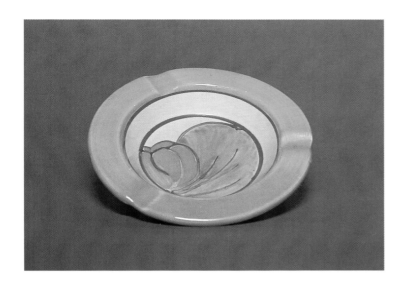

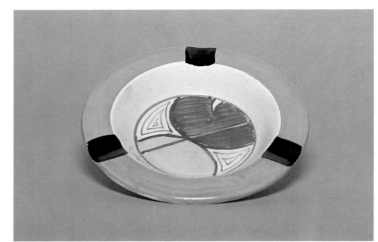

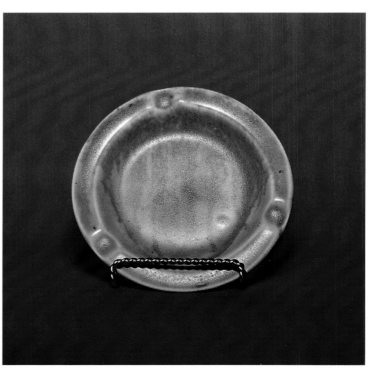

Miscellaneous

This category includes a wide variety of items such as candleholders, table-centerpieces, baskets, nut dishes, masks, sabots, and wall plaques. The range here is obviously wide; however, the starting price is $300 and extends to several thousand.

These mugs utilize the bright Clarice Cliff colors in bands of varying thicknesses. *Collection of Carole A. Berk, Ltd.* Medium

Dame Laura Knight's ladies crowd together on this mug. *Collection of Carole A. Berk, Ltd.* NP

Two of the more sedate designs by Clarice Cliff are shown here on glasses: *Nemesia* and *Goldstone*. *Collection of Carole A. Berk, Ltd.* Low

A luncheon set with a cruise theme by Dame Laura Knight. The *Clarice Cliff* mark can be seen on the cup. *Collection of Carole A. Berk, Ltd.* NP

A 3-inch egg cup is seen here with a diamond geometric pattern. *Collection of Carole A. Berk, Ltd.* Low+

Cottages contribute to many of Clarice Cliff's designs, but this cottage stands alone. *Collection of Carole A. Berk, Ltd.* NP

This *Appliqué* basket (with a close-up of the detail) has the appearance of wicker. *Courtesy of CARA Antiques.* Medium to High

These small nut dishes comprise part of a set in the *Mountain* design. *Collection of Carole A. Berk, Ltd.* Medium for set

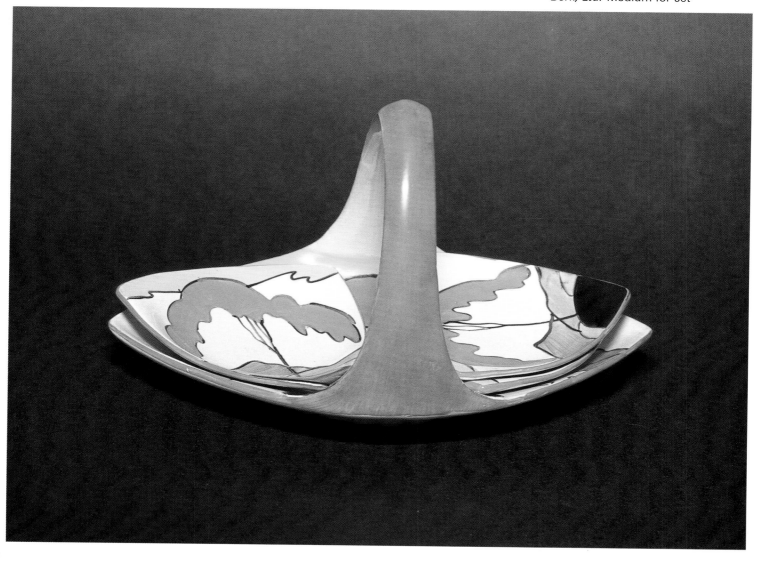

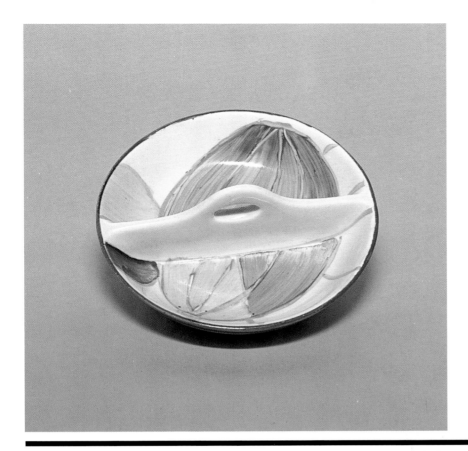

This 4.5-inch divided dish displays a *Fantasque Melon* design. *Collection of Carole A. Berk, Ltd.* Low

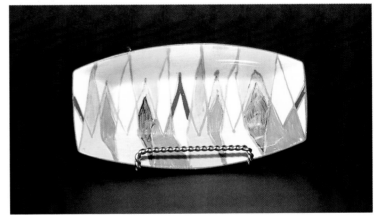

Note the contrasts: the small flowers of the *Nemesia* pattern appear on the large (5.5" x 12") oblong dish, while the larger scale geometrics of *Sungold* counterpoint the small oblong (3" x 5.75") dish. *Collection of Carole A. Berk, Ltd.* Low

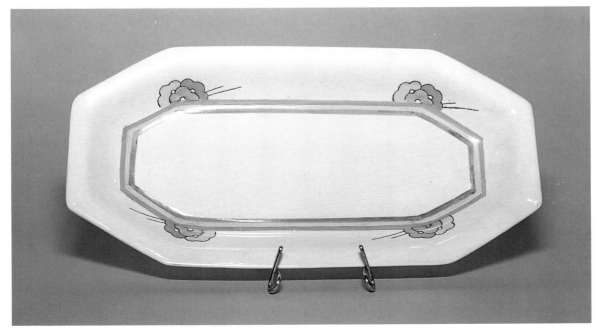

These two small dishes both have a floral design on the stippled *Cafe-au-Lait* ground. *Collection of Carole A. Berk, Ltd.* Low

Both the interior and the exterior of this large (11" diameter) table-center utilize the *Delecia* pattern. *Collection of Carole A. Berk, Ltd.* Medium

This *Bizarre* set includes a curving table-center for flowers, a candleholder, and a dish all with the *Delecia* runnings. *Collection of Carole A. Berk, Ltd*. Medium for set

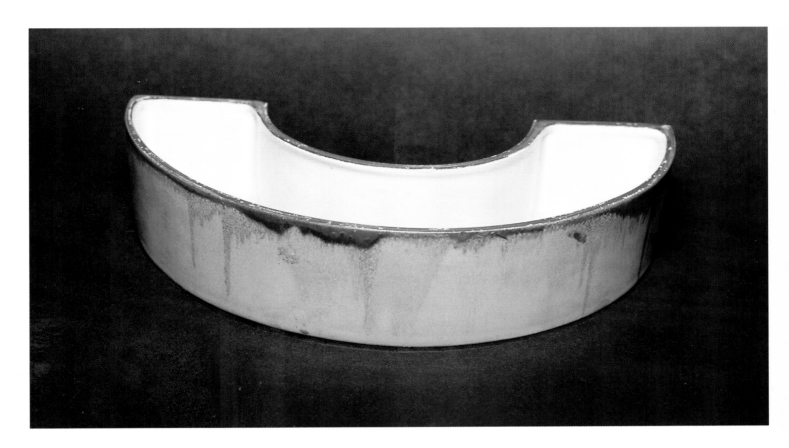

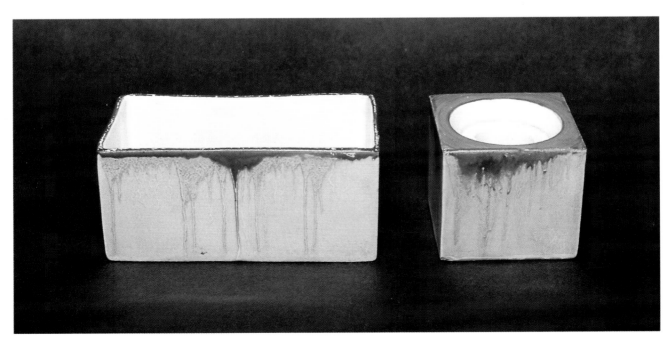

Blue Chintz is the pattern on this candleholder. *Collection of Carole A. Berk, Ltd.* Medium

These *My Garden* candleholders are 5.5" in height. *Collection of Carole A. Berk, Ltd*. Low

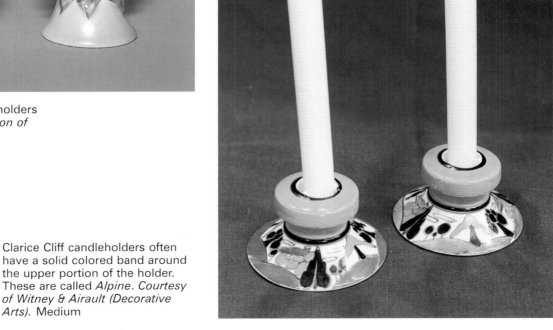

Clarice Cliff candleholders often have a solid colored band around the upper portion of the holder. These are called *Alpine. Courtesy of Witney & Airault (Decorative Arts).* Medium

Latona Red Roses (1930-1931) are quite stylized. Here they are shown on a candleholder. *Collection of Carole A. Berk, Ltd*. Low

Wallmasks were popular in the 1930s. Clarice Cliff produced several different faces, each given the name of a lady. Some appeared on the market in more than one size. *Collection of Carole A. Berk, Ltd.* NP

Clarice Cliff only designed a few toby jugs. Shown here is the Winston Churchill example. *Collection of Carole A. Berk, Ltd.* NP

Compare this wallmask designed by Goebel with the masks designed by Cliff. *Courtesy of Carol C. Smith, Grandad's Attic, Aberdeen.* NP

Observe the flowers reminiscent of *My Garden* on this floral wall plaque by Clarice Cliff. *Courtesy of Carol C. Smith, Grandad's Attic, Aberdeen.* NP

A grouping of Clarice Cliff examples: *Lorna* jug, *Nasturtium* sugar shaker, *Bon Jour* cruet, *Aurea* sugar shaker, and *Marguerite* jam pot. *Courtesy of Carol C. Smith, Grandad's Attic, Aberdeen.* NP

A collection of Cliff pieces with a *Lynton* shape coffee set in the foreground. *Courtesy of Markov & Beedles.* NP

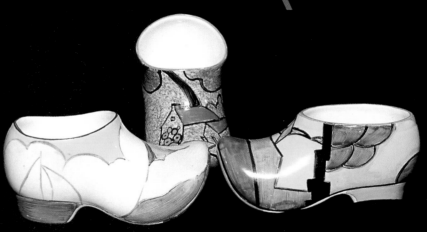

Small shoes in the home are for good luck, so it is not uncommon to find them in a variety of materials and styles. Clarice Cliff chose to shape her production after "sabots" or wooden shoes. Examples here include *Red Roof Cottage, Gibraltar, Sunray,* and *Oranges* on the *Cafe-au-Lait* ground. *Collection of Carole A. Berk, Ltd.* Low to Medium (depending upon design)

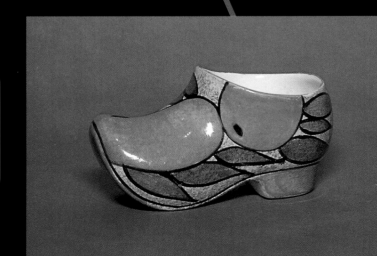

Clarice Cliff designed a series of center-
pieces to be used on the table when
listening to jazz on the radio; consequently,
these *Age of Jazz* figures dance in a "jazzy,"
stylized way. *May Avenue, Antiquarius,
London*. Very Rare

Note the *Bon Jour* shaped tea set in the foreground of this display of Cliff items. *Courtesy of Markov & Beedles.* NP

Serving Pieces by Clarice Cliff make a nice collection. *Courtesy of Carol C. Smith, Grandad's Attic, Aberdeen.* NP

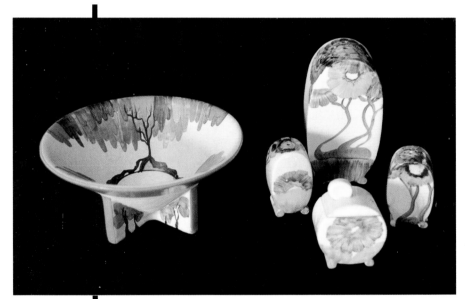

When grouped together, the brightly colored Cliff pieces are hard to miss. *Courtesy of Jonathan Daltrey, Banana Dance.* NP

This collection of globes or spherical vases includes a nice variety of the colors used by Cliff in her many designs. *Collection of Carole A. Berk, Ltd.* NP

Banded mugs complement the tree designs and the early geometric coffee set. *Collection of Carole A. Berk, Ltd.* NP

This limited edition Kevin Francis toby jug is a tribute to Clarice Cliff. Note the *Crocus* design on her chair. *Courtesy of America Toby Jug Museum, Evanston, Illinois.* NP

This Cliff jardiniere looks lovely in an entryway. *Collection of Carole A. Berk, Ltd.* NP

A testament to the popularity of the Cliff designs, reproductions of her most famous patterns are now being used on trays, teawares, and other serving pieces sold in Britain today. NP

Chapter Three
Susie Cooper

Tasteful and Elegant . . .

Like Clarice Cliff, Susan Vera Cooper was born into a large family. Her father had inherited the family farm in Stanfield, near Burslem in the Staffordshire area, from his father. Besides the farm, the Coopers owned several retail businesses such as a grocery store, butchers, and bakery. Although relatively prosperous, after John Cooper's death and the beginning of World War I, a labor shortage existed that forced the family to relocate next to the retail businesses.

Susie, who had attended a public school and preceding that a private school in Hanley, was made to leave school at age fifteen to aid in the family businesses. At sixteen, encouraged by her mother, Susie began to attend evening classes at the Burslem School of Art. Susie particularly seemed to enjoy the plant drawing class she had there, perhaps due in part to her background in farming. In the years to follow, plants emerged as the primary motifs for her natural designs.

It was at the Burslem School of Art that Susie met Gordon Forsyth who became her mentor. Forsyth suggested that Susie attend daytime art classes, which she did. In 1919, she received a full-time scholarship to the school. Having served as the Art Director at Minton Hollins and later at Pilkington Tile and Pottery Company, Forsyth linked area potteries and art. In fact, the Burslem School of Art had a number of his vases on display.

In addition to art, Susie wanted to study fashion design, but to do so she needed a scholarship. The Royal College of Art was offering one, but the applicant had to have experience in the decorative arts. To fulfill this requirement, Forsyth obtained a position for Susie at A. E. Gray & Co. Ltd. Though, after joining Gray's, Susie decided to stay with ceramic design rather than seek a career in fashion design. Edward Gray recognized Susie's talent, and he, like Forsyth, also became her mentor.[1]

Susie Cooper began her career at Gray's Pottery in Hanley, England. *Courtesy of Lorraine Donnelly Art Deco Ceramics.*

The backstamp for Gray's pottery during this period included a ship on waves along with the factory name. Edward's father, Robert Doughty Gray, had been an officer in Her Majesty's Customs, serving aboard a cutter and later a battleship. Edward himself worked as a salesman for a wholesale firm in Manchester, but his doubts about the products he sold inspired the idea of owning a pottery factory.[2] After Susie began to decorate ware for the British Industries Fair of 1923, the backstamp changed to include "designed by Susie Cooper." Edward Gray heralded this trend, much in keeping with the Art Deco idea of limited editions and designer labels. The names of Clarice Cliff and Charlotte Rhead later appeared on pottery in order to promote it.

For the 1923 Fair, one of Susie's primary responsibilities included painting lions on a lusterware called *Gloria Lustre*. (These original luster pieces are extremely hard to find on the open market.) Perhaps this lion paved the way for the leaping deer that became Susie's trademark. While at Gray's, Susie painted geometrics such as *Moon and Mountain*, banded ware, and florals. These brightly-colored ceramics appealed to the consumers. *Cubist* was another popular geometric pattern designed by Susie for Gray's. *The Pottery Gazette* of 1928 described the *Cubist* design as "blobs of colour, and streaks, with blues, greens and reds violently contrasted."[3]

As Susie tired of the restrictions imposed by the sales department as well as the limited shapes available to her, she entertained thoughts of having her own factory. While at Gray's, Susie designed a few shapes, one of which acted as a precursor to the *Kestrel* shape. It was this desire to design new shapes and to establish a clearer connection between form and function that led Susie Cooper to leave Gray's. With her brother-in-law, called "Uncle Jack" Beeson, and her family's support, Susie established a shop in Tunstall. Gordon Forsyth introduced Susie to Albert G. Richardson, a potter from Crown Ducal. Richardson and six paintresses comprised Susie's staff.

The George Street Pottery unfortunately ran into difficulties not long after opening. The same week she left Gray's to start her own business, the Wall Street Crash occurred, causing her landlord to go bankrupt. Susie then moved to Burslem where she rented space in the Chelsea Works from Royal Doulton. Buying whiteware from Grimwades Ltd. and from W. H. Grindley and Company, Susie designed simple patterns such as the *Polka Dot*, the banded patterns, and the

Exclamation Mark, each easy designs for her unskilled paintresses. "The Ladies of the Potteries," as they came to be called, eventually earned much recognition.

Susie aimed to market affordable, tasteful wares to consumers with limited budgets. The first advertisement for the Susie Cooper Pottery appeared in the *Pottery Gazette and Glass Trade Review* in April of 1930: "Elegance combined with Utility, Artistry associated with Commerce and Practicability, truly a strong combination." Later, *Elegance* also became a pattern name. In addition to the advertisement, Susie Cooper was highly praised in an article that stated: "It is only rarely in the history of the Staffordshire Potteries that one comes across an instance of a pottery artist, and particularly a lady, who has the confidence and courage to attempt to carve out a career by laying down a special plant and staff on what must be admitted to be something suggestive of a commercial scale."[4]

As the company began receiving orders from retailers, Susie extended her range of wares to include smoking paraphernalia, like ashtrays and cigarette boxes, nursery ware, vases, lamp bases, and candleholders. In order to keep up with their demand, Susie arranged with Wood and Sons for a supply of good quality whiteware.

The designs Susie exhibited at the 1931 British Industries Fair caused Harry Wood of Wood and Sons to offer Susie and her company space in his Crown Works in Burslem. Here she designed studio ware with incised decoration and nursery ware. Besides incised animals, she designed natural patterns like leaves and acorns.

In 1932, Susie exhibited at the British Industries Fair and it was here that Queen Mary purchased her first tea set. The Queen later confided this point to Susie as she presented her with the Order of the British Empire (OBE) in 1979.

At the Fair, a department store representative bought a range of wares called *Polka Dot.* Following this order, other department stores began ordering Susie Cooper Pottery. Because of these connections and because she regularly promoted her designs, Susie's name became a household word. Perhaps, this is due in part to the advertising phrase credited to Albert Beeson, Susie's brother-in-law and business partner: "No home is complete without Susie Cooper Pottery."[5]

Susie remained involved with all aspects of her company; consequently, the quality remained consistent. Her company continued to grow and she employed forty paintresses. Export orders arrived from as far away as Australia, South Africa, and North America, and special products were designed especially for these overseas markets: Americans bought her Thanksgiving Turkey platter, while Canadians loved her banded wares. In 1940, Susie, now a married woman, received the coveted award of *Royal Designer for Industry*; she remains the first and only woman from The Potteries to receive such an honor.

Branching into other ventures, Susie planned to produce a line of children's clothes. However, the Second World War halted these plans. Shortages caused by the War, coupled with a fire at the Crown Works, caused Susie to stop all production until after wartime. Once the war ended, the factory reopened. In 1946, Susie received an invitation to serve on a committee for an exhibition at the Victoria and Albert Museum; this invitation was perhaps a foreshadowing to her own exhibition held there several decades later in 1987.

By 1950, Susie purchased Jason China Company and added china to the company's products. At this time, new shapes like *Quail* appeared, though the products still retained naturalistic designs. Because the demand for pottery had declined, the introduction of china was fortuitous. Tableware was promoted as giftware, a creative marketing concept. By 1957, Susie Cooper Pottery had 250 employees, and, in 1961, the factory merged with R. H. & S. L. Plant. In 1966, both companies were purchased by Josiah Wedgwood and Sons Limited.

The City Museum and Art Gallery in Stoke-on-Trent held an exhibition in 1982 honoring Susie Cooper on her eighteenth birthday, and, in 1987, Susie was awarded an honorary doctorate from the Royal College of Art. She retired in 1986 and moved to the Isle of Man where she lived with her son, Tim. Susie Cooper died on July 28, 1995.

In the August 1, 1995 issue of *The Independence*, Kathy Niblett, Director of the City Museum and Art Gallery in Stoke-on-Trent, wrote the following in an article honoring Susie Cooper: "There is no one to fill the shoes of Susie Cooper. Her contribution is unique. No one's work compares with hers, either for its ground-breaking technical improvements, for its practicality, for its elegance or for its far-sightedness" (10).

The Designs

As mentioned, due to Susie's agricultural background, her designs rely heavily on natural elements and fundamental patterns. Leaves, grass, feathers, dandelions, and other organic elements became her staples. Other designs, such as exclamation marks, dots, and crescents, are sometimes referred to as "ceramic Morse code."

During her early years at Gray's, Susie utilized the bright colors of the 1920s. Her "Blythe Blue," "Pale Mixed Green," and "Jaffa Orange" often appeared accompanied by black bands and highlighted by "spots" and zigzags in well-defined brushstrokes. Many of Susie's early designs had no names, simply numbers. As is the case with other wares, collectors "nicknamed" the designs for reference and the names have stuck. *Moon and Mountain* is a perfect example of this.

Although her colors changed with the times and by the 1930s some patterns had only pinks and greens, many of the more intense colors remained popular in a variety of ways over the years. Tube-lining, a technique used in The Potteries since prior to the turn of the century (for further information see Chapter Five), and one which Susie adapted with her usual expertise, caught on and other manufacturers utilized the concept with great success. Even today factories still use this method to create fine, hand-painted designs. First, the decorator traces the design onto biscuit ware by means of rubbing charcoal over small holes punched along the outline of a tracing called a pounce. Then, the decorator uses a syringe-type utensil to trail wet slip (or liquid clay) along the outline. The slip leaves a raised outline for the paintresses, who simply fill it in with the colors. In the final stages, the piece goes to the kiln for firing, and is then glazed and refired. The outlined pattern makes the process easier for the less-skilled paintresses.

Polka Dots, one of Susie's early designs, provided jobs for all her employees. The dots were put on by hand, and the young, unskilled paintresses were good at dots. The saucers had reverse

Both Clarice Cliff and Susie Cooper worked for Wedgwood at some point in their careers, as did Keith Murray. Shown here is the entrance to the Wedgwood Museum and the statue of Josiah Wedgwood that stands in the courtyard. *Courtesy of Josiah Wedgwood & Sons Ltd.*

dots, requiring them to be painted first and the spots made by removing the paint. Cooper herself commented that the pattern was "useful to us, because we trained the paintresses on it. It taught them to grind and handle colour, and, instead of having to wipe everything off and start again, once they reached a level of proficiency the items could be fired." Susie did insist that the dots be consistent though. Another training pattern was the *Exclamation Mark*. Additionally, Susie also designed complicated patterns for her more skilled laborers.

One of Susie Cooper's most popular designs was the *Dresden Spray*. Sold in both pink and green, a morning set with nine pieces originally sold for 46p (pence). An entire dinner set, which included a tea and breakfast set, sold for nearly eight pounds sterling. Edward VIII, in fact, bought a pink version for Wallace Simpson.[6]

In 1952, wartime restrictions on decorations were lifted, so more color appeared. The designs of the 1960s, the pop culture in vogue, utilized an idea of mixing and matching sets. For example, a set of cups and saucers with similar patterns of various colors or designs could be mixed and matched so any cup matched any saucer. One of the best selling patterns from the 1960s exemplifying this concept was *Contrast*, aptly named. Susie was enthralled with the scenes on Carnaby Street and even named a design *Carnaby Daisy.*

Susie Cooper's most successful designs for Wedgwood included *Glen Mist* and *Corn Poppy.* Wedgwood also produced a range of Susie's patterns with Egyptian inspirations to coincide with the King Tutankhamen Show in London. One such pattern was *Ashmun.* In addition, Susie designed ranges inspired by other artistic dynasties like the Chou Dynasty. The Western Han Dynasty, symbolized by "Tiger Cubs in Combat with Wild Boar," was yet another civilization that inspired some of Susie's designs. These thematic wares used a simulated lithograph on plastic that was absorbed by the glaze as it melted in the kiln. This "lithograph" with its cut out shapes acted as a textured covercoat. "Prestige Ware by Susie Cooper" seems an appropriate name for such creativity.

In 1977, *Classic Vista* was selected for the Silver Jubilee. Susie's husband, Cecil Barker, an architect by vocation, had helped to create this design which first appeared in pattern books in 1959. His architectural input is displayed most prominently in the design by the columns in the foreground with well-proportioned buildings behind them.

One of the last Cooper designs by Wedgwood appeared in 1986 as a reproduction of the earlier *Kestrel* shape with 1930s designs of *Spiral Fern, Daisy,* and *Polka Dots.* Just recently, Wedgwood reproduced Cooper's silver luster in limited quantities; originally, it was one of Susie's first designs for Gray's Pottery. These limited editions have a waiting list.

Susie Cooper's technical achievements include translucent bone china, in-glaze decoration whereby the design is sandwiched between two layers of glaze for protection, and lithographic transfer prints that closely resemble hand-painted designs.[7]

Britain, as one would expect, has many collectors who appreciate Susie Cooper. Furthermore, in recent years, Japanese consumers have shown much interest in designs by Susie Cooper, especially designs embellished with pink flowers. Today, the market in the United States is steadily growing as more and more people become aware of the technical expertise and clever practicality exhibited by this talented entrepreneur.

The logo for Susie Cooper Pottery became the leaping deer, a form that appeared as a centerpiece for the table in 1936 and 1937. Thereafter, leaping deer have appeared in various designs over the years. Cooper herself once commented that the "poor deer" seemed doomed to continually dart across her pottery.

The Shapes

Susie Cooper's genius reached beyond patterns. She designed shapes that did more than simply appeal to the eye: they were well-engineered. Unlike Clarice Cliff's examples, Susie Cooper's teapots poured properly, and the handles remained cool. Besides shapes, Susie was also technically innovative. She began aerographing, or spray painting, the colors onto the ware. Sgraffito is another method Susie rejuvenated. Though sgraffito is an ancient technique for putting designs into pottery by cutting away the color, Susie used this method to create more complicated designs.

The shapes of Susie Cooper teapots and coffee services changed over the years. Early earthenware shapes like *Kestrel* and *Curlew* (1932) became more streamlined with curves inverted to form the *Falcon* shape of the following year. The *Rex* and the *Classic* shapes were streamlined versions of existing shapes. The *Fluted* shape along with the *Quail* (1950*)* shape appeared on the market in china patterns.

Falcon

Quail

Kestrel

Rex

Another famous shape created by Susie Cooper is the *Can* shape. Created in 1957 as a shape for bone china, the *Can* shape has remained in constant production since that time. As the name indicates, the outline is cylindrical just like a can.

Besides these shapes, Susie Cooper created a vegetable dish with a lid that has a flat center area. This enabled the lid to be set upright on the table so the steam would not roll onto the tablecloth. Concepts like this one earned her tableware lines the reputation of practicality.

Can

Pitchers and Jugs

Susie's designs for pitchers range from the early luster to the geometrics, like *Moon and Mountain,* to incised studio ware, to *Short Order* jugs. The price range averages from $100 to several hundred. Since the older geometric patterns are quite collectible, these designs fall into the higher range.

Painted in enamel colors, this geometric *Moon and Mountains* jug, 4.5" in height, was made in the *Paris* shape for A. E. Gray & Co. Ltd., c.1928. *Courtesy of Lorraine Donnelly Art Deco Ceramics.* Medium to High

Hand-painted floral patterns on a plain ground were manufactured in the early 1930s. Compare these flowers to the *Azalea* pattern of the 1960s. *Courtesy of Nick Jones, Susie Cooper Ceramics.* NP

From 1932 to 1938, Susie Cooper designed studio wares for Wood & Sons Ltd. These incised designs expressed a great deal of movement, whether with animal figures like that of the 1932 *Stag* (E325) displayed on the larger pitcher, or with foliage like that of *Acorn* (E324). *Courtesy of Plum's Emporium, Toronto.* Low

Teaware and Coffee Services

The majority of Susie Cooper's productions consisted of tableware, and she is perhaps most well-known for her teaware and coffee services. The shapes of her pots quickly identify them as Cooper. Unlike Clarice Cliff's attractive yet impractical designs, Cooper's serving pots were carefully engineered. Their handles stayed cool while the liquid poured easily and quickly, making serving safer. The price range for the items in this category varies considerably, depending on the combination of shape and design as well as the number of pieces in the set. Prices quoted here are for one piece unless otherwise noted.

The low end of the range is under $100. Usually cups and saucers fall into this category. Serving pieces often fall into the higher range. Complete sets can range well into the thousands.

Probably made for the American market, this *Short Order* fisherman jug is unpretentious in its simplicity. *Courtesy of Plum's Emporium, Toronto.* Medium

From 1932 to 1934, these elaborate shapes delighted the consumer. *Courtesy of Nick Jones, Susie Cooper Ceramics.* NP

A 1932 pattern called *Nosegay* covers this tea set. *May Avenue, Antiquarius, London*. High+ for set

This *Kestrel* coffee set with bands was made in the early 1930s. *May Avenue, Antiquarius, London*. Medium (set without plates)

Cooper often looked to nature as an inspiration for her designs. This array of serving pieces illustrates her patterns based on shapes found in the landscape. *Courtesy of Nick Jones, Susie Cooper Ceramics.* NP

The coffee set appeared on the market in a variety of color combinations. *Courtesy of Plum's Emporium, Toronto.* Low (per piece)

Shown here is a 1938 aerographed coffee set with a sgraffito design. *Courtesy of Nick Jones, Susie Cooper Ceramics.* High (for complete set)

Some of Susie Cooper's popular designs, such as *Swansea Spray, Patricia Rose, and Grey Leaf,* appeared on coffee pots. *Courtesy of Lorraine Donnelly Art Deco Ceramics.* NP

The 1935 design *Swansea Spray* (shown here) became *Printemps* when scalloped borders were added to the design. The lithographed design, *Patricia Rose,* was manufactured for 40 years. *Courtesy of Lorraine Donnelly Art Deco Ceramics.* Low

Manufactured in a variety of colors, the lithographed *Dresden Spray* became one of Susie Cooper's most popular designs. *Courtesy of Lorraine Donnelly Art Deco Ceramics*. Low

Elegance, a transfer print design, first manufactured in the late 1930s and later in the 1950s, is shown here on the *Falcon* shape. As with other patterns, the design came in a variety of color combinations. *Courtesy of Plum's Emporium, Toronto*. Low

Banding appeared in a variety of ways and colors. Note the color-coordinated interiors. *Courtesy of Plum's Emporium, Toronto*. Low

This design was one on display at the British Industry Fair in 1947. Cooper often used dot arrangements like *Starburst, Asterix, Raised Dots, Crescents, Diamonds*, and the like in her pattern designs. *Courtesy of Plum's Emporium, Toronto*. Low

Susie Cooper's floral patterns, as well as fruit and berry designs, appeared on her china of the 1950s. *Courtesy of Plum's Emporium, Toronto*. Low

The *Quail* shape coffee and tea services shown here are decorated in *Polka Dot*, a later version for china of the earlier *Raised Spot* design. *Courtesy of Plum's Emporium, Toronto*. Low (per piece)

Popular shapes from the mid 1950s and the 1960s include the *Can* shape, both for pots and for cups. This set dates to around 1969. The *Can* shape, originated by Susie Cooper, became a most enduring shape. *Courtesy of Plum's Emporium, Toronto*. Low

A *Can* shape shown with a *Whispering Grass* cup and saucer of a similar color. *Courtesy of Plum's Emporium, Toronto.* Low

Browns were frequently used for decorating bone china in the 1960s. Shown here are *Can* shaped cups and saucers in a variety of brown designs, including the popular *Diablo* with its hourglass brown and black pattern. *Courtesy of Plum's Emporium, Toronto.* Low

From single bands to flowers to the 1964 *Persia* pattern, these bone china pieces depict some of the designs Cooper did for Wedgwood. *Courtesy of Plum's Emporium, Toronto.* Low

Right:
Produced for Wedgwood in the mid 1960s, the *Corinthian* design makes use of a brown and black combination popular at the time. *Courtesy of Plum's Emporium, Toronto.* Low

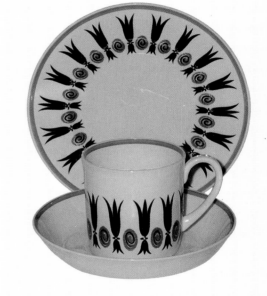

Venetia was a design manufactured on bone china from 1964 to 1966. *Courtesy of Plum's Emporium, Toronto.* Low

Classic Vista was one of the most intricate of the Cooper designs for Wedgwood bone china, first appearing in pattern books in 1959. It became most popularly associated with the England's Silver Jubliee. *May Avenue, Antiquarius, London.* Rare to find complete service for 8.

Other 1960s designs seen on Wedgwood bone china include the *Apple Gay* pattern of 1964. *Courtesy of Plum's Emporium, Toronto.* Low

These photos show a medley of teapots and coffeepots, indicating the diversity of the Cooper designs. *Courtesy of Nick Jones, Susie Cooper Ceramics.* NP

Plates

Susie Cooper plates offer a wide range for the collector. The early plates from the years associated with Gray's Pottery have bright, often floral, designs in contrast to the later studio wares with incised decoration. Her rectangular cocktail plates complement the aerographed and sgraffito patterns. Banded designs come in a variety of colors. Some collectors choose pieces from a particular period, while others concentrate on acquiring all items within a particular range or design. The Dynasty patterns make for an interesting and eye-catching display.

Prices for the plates begin at under $100 for the more common designs and extend to several hundred for the more collectible examples.

Designed for A. E. Gray around 1928, this brightly colored, enameled design was intended to compete with the Czechoslovakian imports of the period. *Courtesy of Plum's Emporium, Toronto.* Medium

Other designs done in enamels carried more subtle colors. *Courtesy of Plum's Emporium, Toronto.* Medium

From 1932 to 1938, studio wares included such patterns as this tulip design, shown here on dessert plates. *Courtesy of Plum's Emporium, Toronto.* Medium

The ever-popular rose designs are seen here with different borders. *Courtesy of Nick Jones, Susie Cooper Ceramics.* NP

After World War II, production problems encouraged the implementation of hand-painted patterns rather than lithographic transfers. These free-hand designs included the *Pear in Pompadour* (shown here) as well as the *Tulip in Pompadour. Courtesy of Nick Jones, Susie Cooper Ceramics.* Medium

Other designs from the 1940s include the frequently used leaves and flowers, but with a slightly different treatment. Here, they are done in sgraffito on an aerographed ground. *Courtesy of Plum's Emporium, Toronto.* Low+

The leaping deer, shown here on a plate, received a variety of treatments over the years, becoming synonymous with Susie Cooper's ceramics. *Courtesy of Plum's Emporium, Toronto.* Low+

These 1940s cocktail plates utilize zigzag lines, seen on other Cooper designs, in unique ways. *Courtesy of Plum's Emporium, Toronto.* Low+

Miscellaneous

Since Susie Cooper concentrated on designing tasteful tableware for the consumer with a limited budget, her miscellaneous items often attract the collector. Items such as bowls, vases, mugs, and toast racks make for variety within a collection.

The price range for this group begins under $100 and goes upward. A vase in a collectible design averages several hundred.

The matt glaze studio vases of the 1930s highlight the circular lines used by Cooper in her painted designs. The simpler lines of the later vases utilize circles completely around the vases as structural decoration. *Courtesy of Plum's Emporium, Toronto.* Medium

The incised squirrel design in this studio piece (1932-1938) repeats the circular motions seen in many of the Cooper patterns. *Courtesy of Plum's Emporium, Toronto.* Medium

Banded mugs of the 1930s were decorated in enamels Susie Cooper named "chrome green," "blythe blue," and "silver yellow" and were often combined with black. Later mugs added scallops, dots, or zigzag lines. *Courtesy of Plum's Emporium, Toronto.* Medium

A *Florida* beaker with bands on the upper interior rim. *Courtesy of Plum's Emporium, Toronto.* Low

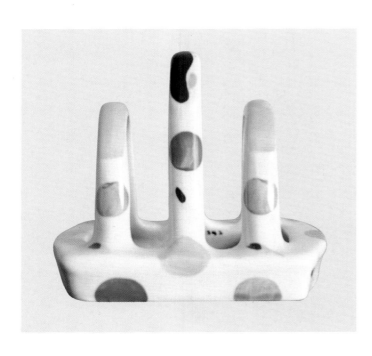

Toast racks were fashionable pieces for the breakfast tables of the 1930's and 1940's. The Cooper greens and yellow here are combined with black as they were on other items. *Courtesy of Lorraine Donnelly, Art Deco Ceramics.* Low

The diversity of Susie Cooper decorations on plates and cups attests to the creativity of her designs. *Courtesy of Nick Jones, Susie Cooper Ceramics.* NP

This limited edition Kevin Francis toby jug represents Susie Cooper. Collectors of Cliff, Cooper, and Rhead frequently round out their collections with the Kevin Francis tributes to the respective designers. *Courtesy of the American Toby Jug Museum, Evanston, Illinois.* NP

Chapter Four

Keith Murray

An Architect at Heart . . .

Born in New Zealand in 1892, Keith Murray attended King's College in Auckland, followed by Mill Hill School in London. After serving in the Royal Flying Corps during World War I, where he received the Military Cross and Croix de Guerre Belge, Murray studied architecture.[1] Unfortunately, just as he was beginning his career, the depression of the early 1930s peaked, and suddenly he was unemployed. Faced with finding other work, Murray, having been a collector of glass for many years, had the good fortune of be-

This *Moonstone* glaze bowl by Keith Murray measures 7" in diameter and 4" in height. *Collection of Carole A. Berk, Ltd. Medium*

ing introduced to Arthur Marriot Powell, one of the directors of Whitefriars Glassworks. Powell became a mentor for Murray and produced a few of his designs.

By 1932, Murray was employed as a glass designer at Stevens and Williams Glassworks of Brierley Hill. There, under the direction of Herbert Williams-Thomas, Murray designed on a freelance basis. Having attended the 1925 Art Deco Show in Paris, Murray found himself attracted to the sleek, Swedish glass designs. This interest in modernism remained with him throughout his various careers. Much of the glassware of the period consisted of highly decorated, fanciful designs. Murray's modernistic forms with their understated practicality caught the attention of the critics.

The year 1939 saw the end of his work with Stevens and Williams. At this time, Powell introduced Murray to Felton Wreford, manager of Wedgwood's London Showrooms. Thus began an association that mutually benefited both parties. Wedgwood sought to produce fewer and simpler shapes because of the wartime decrease of exports, especially to America. With his interest in form following function, Murray searched for an outlet besides glass. Pottery provided Murray with the medium in which to learn a new process and keep an eye toward designing items appropriately engineered for the capabilities of the production facilities. It was Murray's training as an architect perhaps that forced him to consider

Glazed with celadon satin, this large bowl has the initials for Keith Murray on the Wedgwood backstamp. *Collection of Carole A. Berk, Ltd.* Medium to High

the method of production, to design a piece for maximum use of the facilities. Murray went to work for Wedgwood as a designer for three months each year.

Wedgwood, known for its classical heritage, found that Murray's contemporary designs gave them the needed change in direction. While at Wedgwood, Murray designed sleek, distinctive wares for consumers with taste but a limited budget, a consumer market in which Susie Cooper also found success.

The designs Murray produced were well-received by the press. Murray was awarded the *Royal Designer for Industry* in 1936, the same award Susie Cooper would receive four years later. Moreover, in 1934, the Royal Silversmiths, Mappin and Webb, invited Murray to design silverplate wares for them.[2] In 1936, Keith Murray acquired a partner, Charles S. White, and opened an architectural firm. Wedgwood commissioned Murray's firm to design a new facility at the Barlaston factory.

Prior to 1940, wares designed by Murray carried the full signature; after that date, however, wares only displayed his initials along with the Wedgwood mark. Murray left Wedgwood in 1946, but the company continued to produce his designs until 1950. In 1967, Murray retired from his practice. Merely eleven years later, the Victoria and Albert Museum honored Keith Murray with an exhibition of his work. He died in May of 1981.

Above and right: Murray's matt straw bowl carries his full signature backstamp, indicating the piece was made prior to 1941. After that time, only his initials were used on the backstamp. *Collection of Carole A. Berk, Ltd.* Medium

Designs, Shapes, and Glazes

Matt glazes and classic shapes with simple lines demonstrate Keith Murray's most desirable and collectible wares. Matt white, called *Moonstone*, was first to appear on the market, but matt straw, matt green, matt gray, and turquoise closely followed. These "Siennese" glazes allowed the form of the piece to prevail. Though sometimes designed with outward or inverted ridges, few of Murray's wares have decoration. Rare examples of Murray's designs include those produced in black or brown basalt.

The price range for Murray items is quite wide. Smaller items may be as little as one hundred dollars, while larger, more collectible vases may cost several thousand dollars. For the sake of a price range, prices run as follows: Low: $100 to $500; Medium: $800 to $2,000; High: $2,000 and up.

The basalt vase, reminiscent of the basalt for which Wedgwood became famous, makes a nice contrast to the *Moonstone* glaze pieces in this display of Keith Murray pieces. Black basalt items are among the rarest of the Murray wares. *May Avenue, Antiquarius, London.* Rare

While some Keith Murray vases have the inverted bands as architectural decoration, others have the raised ridges. Both of these pieces are 7" in height. *Collection of Carole A. Berk, Ltd.* Medium

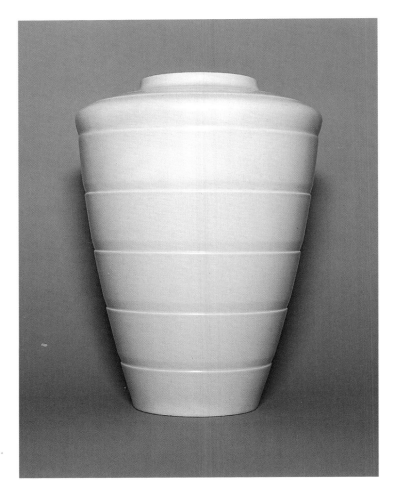

Shoulder vases appeared on the market in a variety of Murray colors, including the matt straw and matt blue. *Collection of Carole A. Berk, Ltd.* High

Besides matt glazes, Murray also used a semi-matt white *Moonstone* glaze, shown here on a 9.5-inch *Ridge* vase. *Collection of Carole A. Berk, Ltd*. Low to Medium

Above and left:
The vertical lines on these matt green vases nicely contrast the diagonal lines of the fluted design. *Collection of Carole A. Berk, Ltd*. Medium and Low respectively

Above and right:
These *Ridge* vases came
in matt green and matt
straw glazes, such as
these 8-inch vases.
*Collection of Carole A.
Berk, Ltd*. Low to Medium

Similar to the *Ridge* design but slightly smaller, this vase has inverted bands. *Collection of Carole A. Berk, Ltd.* Low

Shown here is a celadon satin glaze on a recognizable Murray shape, 8" in height. *Collection of Carole A. Berk, Ltd*. Medium

Small *Weathervane* vases by Keith Murray appear more decorated than many of his designs. *Collection of Carole A. Berk, Ltd.* Low

Other designers used matt glazes similar to those by Keith Murray. This cigarette box (note the design on the lid) is Wedgwood Etruria, but was not designed by Murray. *Collection of Carole A. Berk, Ltd.* NP

The gentle curve and inverted band design make it is easy to recognize these mugs as designed by Keith Murray. *Collection of Carole A. Berk, Ltd.* Low

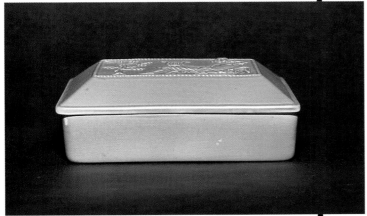

The *Persian Rose* design (pattern number 4040) shown here on a 9-inch jug was probably influenced by the designs of William Morris and dates from about 1927. *Collection of Carole A. Berk, Ltd.* Medium

Born into a Family of Potters . . .

Frederick Alfred Rhead trained at Mintons as a designer under Louis Solon. He achieved the position of Art Director at Wileman & Co., but moved to accept the same position at Wood & Sons in 1913. Along with his brother, George Woolliscroft Rhead, Frederick co-wrote *Staffordshire Pots and Potters*.

On October 19, 1885, Frederick and his French wife had their fourth child, Charlotte Antoinette Adolphine. "Lottie," as she was called, became seriously ill and housebound at the age of seven. Soon after she returned to the outdoors, she fell and broke her leg. Although it healed, the leg remained shorter than the other, leaving Charlotte with a pronounced limp. Over time, she learned to walk normally, but by then she had fallen behind the other children in learning. Perhaps as a result of these childhood experiences, Charlotte, though cheerful, remained a shy individual.

Shortly after her father began working at Wood & Sons, Charlotte joined him. Having learned painting and drawing from her father, Charlotte now also had the opportunity to observe her father's careful work on pâte-sur-pâte (paste on paste) designs, a process in which decorators form a design by adding layers of slip, or wet clay, upon previously dried layers, requiring much time, patience, and skill. Later, Charlotte tried this process herself.

Charlotte began her career as a tile decorator at T. & R. Boote, a leading manufacturer of tube-lined tiles. Tube-lining was a process originally imported into The Potteries in 1895 by Harry Barnard while he was the director of the Art Pottery Department at Macintyre's in Burslem. One year later, Barnard transferred to Wedgwood's, and there, too, did tube-lining. Already an expensive process to produce, for each added color the cost of tube-lining multiplies. When Wedgwood discontinued this type of decorating, Barnard asked Frederick, still at Wileman's, to employ the laid-off decorators he had trained. In this manner, Wileman's began producing tube-lined wares, and it was there that Charlotte's two brothers worked, who in turn trained their two sisters, Charlotte and Dollie. Charlotte acquired her first job at T. & R. Boote, though it had been her desire to work for Moorcroft.[1]

Frederick Rhead and Harry Wood opened a separate art wares company called Bursley Ltd., the "s" is not pronounced, at the Crown Pottery in Burslem. Charlotte transferred there to decorate the tube-lined articles. In addition, she also decorated at Ellgreave Pottery Co. Ltd. At the age of forty-one, Charlotte was asked to supervise and train the tube-liners of Burgess & Leigh at Middleport Pottery, not far from Crown Pottery. Burgess & Leigh called their line of art wares "Burleigh Ware." Though pronounced the same, the latter is not to be confused with Wood's "Bursley Ware."

Charlotte worked for A. G. Richardson, the manufacturer of "Crown Ducal Ware," from 1931 until 1943. Located first in Tunstall at the Gordon Pottery, Richardson bought the Britannia Pottery at Cobridge in 1934. He relocated his factory there after modernizing it. Charlotte created new tube-lined designs including patterns such as the *Rhodian, Byzantine, Persian Rose, Golden Leaves,* and the *Manchu,* often applied on mottled glazes. She also created a *Stitch* pattern named after embroidery, and she used a thick, white glaze just developed at Richardson's for her *Wisteria* and *Foxglove. The Pottery Gazette and Glass Trade Review* of 1934 highly praised these new products: "A. G. Richardson in their new sample range, have something of everything and for everybody, besides which . . . their wares have definite characteristics such as place them in a class which the retailer can ill afford to lose sight of."[2] These "Fancies," so called because they represented decorative rather than functional ideals, unfortunately fell prey to wartime restrictions.

It was not only these wartime restrictions but also the management difficulties that eventually caused Charlotte to end her employment with Richardson. Shortly thereafter, Harry Wood recruited Charlotte to return to his firm for experimenting with luster glazes. Charlotte Rhead died while still with Wood & Son on November 6, 1947. She was sixty-two years old.

Those who started collecting Charlotte Rhead a few years ago are very fortunate. Because of ample productivity, one could manage to acquire a sizable collection for a reasonable sum on money. Beginning with the 1985 television series entitled, "The Pottery Ladies," however, Charlotte

The double-looped cobalt handle on this *Byzantine* jug accents the cobalt in the flowers. Note the "C Rhead" backstamp. *Collection of Carole A. Berk, Ltd.* Medium

Cobalt grapes hang with golden apples on this lovely Charlotte Rhead vase, 7.5" in height. *Collection of Carole A. Berk, Ltd.* Medium

Rhead's reputation spread. Even though relatively prolific in her career, her original designs attracted the attention of museums and auction houses, which paid tribute by holding exhibitions and special sales, thus launching a trend. Currently, it is still possible to find good buys on Charlotte Rhead pieces, but it is not unreasonable to assume that her wares may follow the path of Clarice Cliff and Susie Cooper.

Marks for Charlotte Rhead's designs are confusing at best. From 1921 until 1929, the ware had the printed mark of "Bursley Ware/England," but no name. In 1923, while at Ellgreave Pottery Co. Ltd., Charlotte used her middle name in print: "Lottie Rhead Ware/Burlsem/England." From 1926 to 1931, some pieces appear with the painted signature "L Rhead," along with the name of the ware: Burleigh Ware or Bursley Ware. Sometimes the initial of the decorator or tubeliner and the number of the pattern also appear. With the Crown Ducal mark, from 1931 to 1943, the "C Rhead" signature occurs with the name of the ware. Since Wood & Son continued to produce wares designed by Charlotte Rhead even after her death, pieces with the printed mark "Bursley Ware/Charlotte Rhead/England" date from 1943 until 1960.[3] As a way to avoid the confusion that both the names of the wares and the name of Charlotte herself present, a good rule of thumb might be: if Charlotte's *full name* appears along with "Bursley Ware," the piece is *not* one of the earlier ones. Many of Charlotte Rhead's designs generally had only pattern numbers, though some ranges were identified by name.

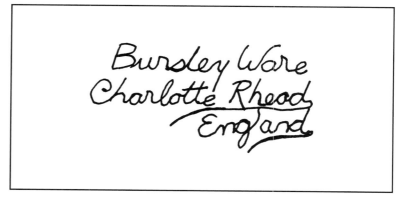

This Rhead mark was stamped on wares from 1943 to 1960. Note: If Charlotte's *full* name appears on the backstamp, it is not one of the early pieces.

Price ranges for Rhead wares average around $400 to $700 for the more common pieces, while the mid-range items cost from $800 to $1,200. The high range begins at around $1,300.

Charlotte Rhead numbered her patterns, but in addition she gave some a name; the design on this jug and on the charger is called *Manchu,* pattern number 4511. Note the detail of the tube-lined decoration. *Collection of Carole A. Berk, Ltd.* Medium

Curving tree trunks like the one shown on this 12-inch charger remind one of the tree in *Bridgewater* by Clarice Cliff. *Courtesy of Nick Jones, Susie Cooper Ceramics.* NP

The Persian influence is obvious on the pattern. A close examination of the detail reveals a careful balancing of colors. The light orange dots accent the same color in the center, while the green draws the eye outward. *May Avenue, Antiquarius, London.* Low

This 12-inch wall plaque is pattern number 4100. *Collection of Carole A. Berk, Ltd*. Low

The leaves of this design create the illusion of movement and draw attention to the orange flowers with touches of green as accents. *Collection of Carole A. Berk, Ltd.* Low

Compare the orange used in this *Orange Oak Leaves* design with the orange in the preceding photos. *May Avenue, Antiquarius, London*. Low

Rhodian (pattern number 3272) is another design that used orange as an accent color. This pattern was popular in 1933. *Collection of Carole A. Berk, Ltd*. Low to Medium

Charlotte Rhead's designs make a colorful display. The bowl design is simply referred to as "yellow and green leaves." *Courtesy of Nick Jones, Susie Cooper Ceramics.* NP

Chapter Six
Carlton Ware

Through the Years . . .

Since Carlton Works opened for business around the time Clarice Cliff, Susie Cooper, Keith Murray, and Charlotte Rhead were born, and closed its doors near the time the last of these designers died, it seems most appropriate to include it in this book. Moreover, the designers at Carlton Ware predicted the market exceedingly well and closely followed the trends in the decorative arts. In many cases, they started a trend by captivating consumers with their original designs. Because Carlton Ware clearly established the parameters for the pottery of this period, a close examination of the output of this innovative factory affords the collector a clearer understanding of the economics of the twentieth century.

After having worked for his father at the James Macintyre & Co. Ltd, James Frederick Wiltshaw sought to open his own pottery works. With the Robinson brothers, James Alcock and William Herbert, he established Carlton Works in 1890 on Stoke's Copeland Street. Originally, the company made wares that were similar to the important products of other factories: a blush like Royal Worcester, sprigged ware similar to Wedgwood's, blue transfer printed ware like Flow Blue, and Imari. Perhaps this remarkable ability to distinguish the most marketable wares and emulate their designs allowed Carlton Works to endure for the better part of a hundred years.

Early Carlton Ware used productions from other factories as inspiration. A *Cactus Flower* vase by Carlton Ware closely resembles the Art Nouveau poppies on the square dish, as well as the gilding and the filigree decoration on the Royal Worcester vase. *Courtesy of C.W.C.I. and St. Clere.* NP

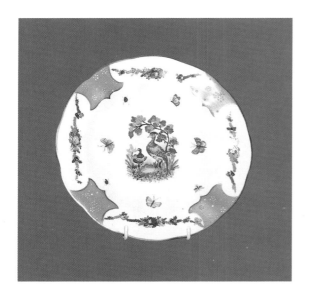

The birds on this Carlton Ware plate (shown here with a plain ware teapot) are remarkably similar to those on the Royal Worcester plate. *Courtesy of C.W.C.I. and St. Clere.* NP

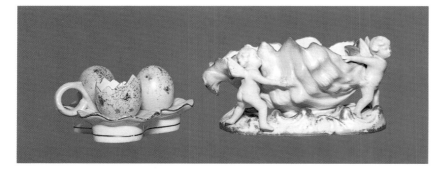

The Renaissance Revival period in Britain during the last quarter of the nineteenth century was reflected in the ceramic arts as well as other decorative arts. Pottery often included cherubs or putti, like those shown on this shell bowl by Carlton. The soft colors and gilding on the egg cruet set also reflect the same time period. *Courtesy of C.W.C.I. and St. Clere.* NP

Carlton's designers were quick to duplicate a trend, but they were always original in their interpretation. These early pieces of Carlton Ware include the *Marguerite* vase in the Imari style, a square dish not unlike Delft, and a *Petunia* teapot that resembles Flow Blue. *Courtesy of C.W.C.I. and St. Clere.* NP

Early examples of Carlton Ware include this *Chintz* box, *Cretonne* vase, and polka dot demitasse cup. *Courtesy of C.W.C.I. and St. Clere.* NP

These early Carlton Ware pieces clearly reflect the Victorian influence. Shown here are a *Chrysanthemum* vase, a tinted faience candleholder, and a sprigged ware vase in the style of Wedgwood. *Courtesy of C.W.C.I. and St. Clere.* NP

Management difficulties at the firm arose as James Robinson's nephew, Harold Taylor Robinson, took over his responsibilities. Eventually, in 1911, James Wiltshaw acquired the firm. Hiring Horace Wain as designer, the firm offered Oriental designs, along with Persian ones, which attracted the attention of the consumer. By the time of the First World War, other creative patterns included birds and blossoms. Chintz designs continued in popularity until around 1920.

In 1918, following the death of his father, James Wiltshaw, Frederick Cuthbert took over the control of the firm. At this time, the company began offering wares designed to compete with the luster items on the market. Calling their products "Lustrous," Carlton Ware advertised them and even displayed them at the British Industrial Arts Fair in 1920, much to their acclaim. These elaborately designed pieces manifested several colors on a mottled ground. Also, because the pieces were fired at a lower temperature, they were cheaper to produce, with the exception of their Armand Lustre Ware. Armand Lustre Ware has a special backstamp consisting of the name of the line encircling two fish.

During the early 1920s, Egyptian wares became quite trendy as a result of the opening of Tutankhamen's tomb. Of course, Carlton Ware did not fail to take advantage of this popularity. Bowls, ashtrays with a raised bust of King Tut, and other similar items were made available and eagerly purchased by consumers.

Enoch Boulton replaced Wain as designer in the early 1920s, launching an extremely productive period in the company's history. By offering innovative new patterns, Boulton took credit for increasing Carlton Ware's market share. During this period, a new backstamp appeared, using a cursive style. Today, collectors refer to it as the "Script Mark." Unlike the earlier "Crown Mark," which consisted of a bird encircled by "W & R Stoke On Trent" with a crown above and the factory name and "Made in England" below, the new mark was much simpler.

During the 1930s and 1940s, Carlton introduced novelty wares in embossed designs. These embossed wares have not only the script mark, but indicate that they are "Registered Australian Design, Registration Applied for." In order to prevent Japan from copying patterns, since at the time England had no trade agreement with Japan, Carlton Ware, to prevent unauthorized use of their designs, sent their wares through Australia, a member of the Commonwealth. The "Australian Wares," as they are called, exhibit a four or five digit impressed number which indicates the mold number and the size. Manufacturers' records number molds as they are designed, and many of these designs were manufactured in several sizes.

Fresh ideas and a new backstamp kept the company at the forefront. Designs such as the *River Fish, Red Devil,* and *Sketching Bird* appealed to a market of eager consumers. Moreover, the popular geometrical designs as well as the fantasy patterns like *Fantasia, New Flies,* and *Fairy* were much sought after by a war-weary public. *Floral Comets, Rainbow Fans*, and *Explosions* seemed to symbolize the exuberance of the period.

As the public tired of the highly glazed items, Carlton Ware led the way in offering consumers "Handcraft" items with a smooth, matt glaze. Also, because the public desired hand-painted items, the firm obliged the demand. Geometrical and floral patterns carried the script backstamp in addition to the words "Handcraft" and "Trade Mark, Made in England." These lines included both urban and rural patterns, from *Metropolis* to *Tree & Swallow*.

The Second World War severely restricted British pottery manufacturers and it was not until Midwinter's Pottery created a range of "Stylecraft" wares that they began to emerge from the slump in sales. Carlton Ware recreated its highly decorated items, but consumers sought the pastels like those Roy Midwinter had created after his visit to America. Carlton Ware's designs like *Windswept* and *Orbit* were in keeping with the New Age of nuclear fusion and space travel. The pylon shape, designed by Philip Forster, seemed appropriate for these new creations.

Without heirs to take over the business, Carlton Works sold out to Arthur Wood Group in 1966. Under the new owners, the factory continued to produce the red and blue ranges, but found that novelty ware regenerated the Carlton Ware market. This success lasted through the 1970s and 1980s, but by the end of that decade, the company went bankrupt.

The Carlton Works remained in operation for nearly 100 years. *Courtesy of C.W.C.I. and St. Clere.*

In the hopes of recreating the splendor of the earlier years at the Carlton Works, John McCluskey of Grosvenor Ceramics purchased the factory records and pattern books. However, after reintroducing the *Rouge Royale* and the *Moonlight Blue* at the Trade Fair in 1992, the company again closed. In 1997, Frank Salmon of Francis Joseph Publications bought the Carlton Works. Currently, he is issuing limited editions of *Hollyhocks,* along with the Carlton Ware figurines. Bairstow Manor Pottery received permission from Salmon to buy many of the original Carlton Ware novelty teapot molds. They are now reintroducing these items.[1]

Novelty Wares

In the mid-1920s, Carlton Ware introduced its tomato and lettuce line of salad ware, but it was the fruit and floral embossed items, with their unusual shapes and delightful colors that the consumers enjoyed beginning in 1935. Today, these items are among the most sought after by collectors. Embossed florals and fruits attract collectors on both sides of the Atlantic and Pacific!

The first embossed design in the factory records is the *Buttercup* in 1935, which was issued in yellow and, less commonly, in pink. *Foxglove* was introduced in 1940. Fruit embossed designs appeared as *Redcurrant, Cherry, Grape, Blackberry,* and *Raspberry*, with the last two being perhaps the most collectible. The embossed ranges generally represented breakfast sets, and one item of particular interest to collectors is the charming, lidded mugs for hot chocolate. Other items appreciated by collectors are the small, leaf-shaped jam or butter dishes with matching spoons.

Collectors also appreciated the novelty teapots made by Carlton Ware. Some resembled bird houses while others had legs. The latter, called *Walking Ware*, is today one of the most sought after of the Carlton Ware products. First introduced in the early 1970s, *Walking Ware* consists of teapots, sugar bowls, and creamers with legs decorated in varieties of stripped, checkered, or polka dot socks. Conceived by Roger Michell and his wife, Danka Napiorkowska, studio potters from Yorkshire, these wares were based on a drawing Danka had done in college. Strangeways Gallery in Chelsea first produced these designs for an annual exhibition in London. Because of the immediate success, however, Roger and Danka needed a manufacturer with greater capacity. Carlton Ware extended a contract and production began.

Based on the success of the original series, which consisted of thirteen pieces, a second series followed. Called Running, Jumping, and Standing Still (RJS), these pieces added a new dimension to the products. Special occasion footed pieces featured extremities for Tarzan and Jane or Santa Claus. Children's mugs and birthday celebrations offered even more variety.

Despite the popularity of these series, Carlton Ware was not able to survive the changing times. Today, using old molds, Arthur Wood Group is reissuing these charming examples.[2]

Reproductions

The Carlton Ware factory closed in 1989 and since that time reproductions with the original backstamp have surfaced. In particular, the Carlton Ware Collectors International reports that the Guinness advertising items like the small animal and the toucan figures have shown up on the market more frequently than the originals. Other reproductions include a small golfing figurine, a mug, and items marked with the Carlton Ware backstamp but never produced by the factory.

As is the case with collecting any type of pottery, knowledge is power. By carefully examining the authentic articles, it becomes easier for the collector to make comparisons. Usually telltale signs, such as incorrect coloring, aid in identification. As mentioned earlier in this book, today's paints have a brighter appearance than the older paints which often contained lead or other toxins. Weight is another sign. Since the clays from various areas differ in content, they also differ in weight. Familiarizing oneself with the genuine articles and lines of production, as well as contacting knowledgeable dealers and collectors, can go a long way in helping to prevent a collector from becoming the target of intended or unintended fraud.

Joining a collectors' group is yet another way of staying informed. The Carlton Ware Collectors International publishes regular newsletters that include the latest news about the factory and its designs, along with up-to-date information on forgeries surfacing in the marketplace. (See the Index of Contributors for the club listing)

Pitchers and Jugs

Carlton Ware pitchers offer real variety for the collector, both in terms of their shape and design. Since the factory produced wares for nearly one hundred years, Carlton offers perhaps more diversity than many of the other twentieth-century factories. From geometrics to tube-lining to embossed wares, Carlton Ware gives collectors a wide variety of choices. The price range for most Carlton Wares runs from just over $100 up to the thousands. For the sake of this text, the "Low" includes wares from under $100 to $250. The "Medium" range averages $300 to $700 and the "High" from $700 to $1,600. Very high items will cost from $1,600 on up.

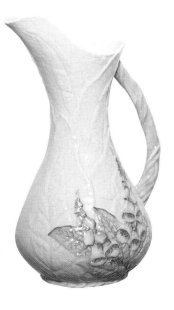

Carlton Ware pitchers appeared on the market in a variety of styles: from the graceful, like this 10-inch floral embossed piece, to the abstract. *Courtesy of C.W.C.I. and St. Clere.* Medium

A 5-inch floral embossed pitcher is shown here with a 4.5-inch fruit embossed preserve pot. *Courtesy of C.W.C.I. and St. Clere.* Low to Medium

A striking 5-inch pitcher, this colorful piece has an opalescent lining. *Collection of Carole A. Berk, Ltd*. Medium

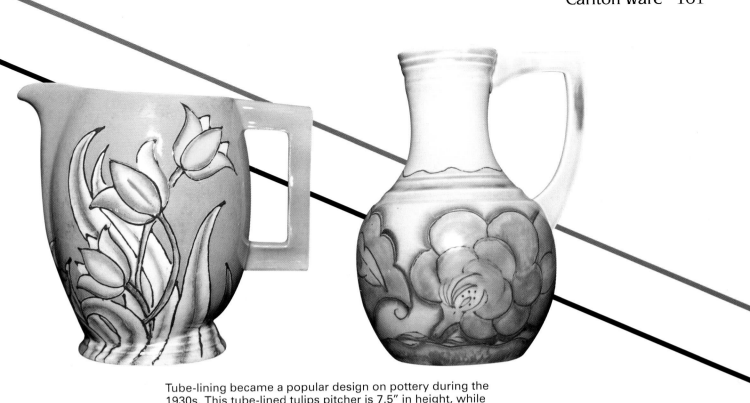

Tube-lining became a popular design on pottery during the 1930s. This tube-lined tulips pitcher is 7.5" in height, while the tube-lined floral jug is 10.5" in height. *Courtesy of C.W.C.I. and St. Clere.* High and Medium respectively

British designers began to market brightly colored pottery to compete with the colorful imports from Czechoslovakia. Shown here is a 7" *Hiawatha* jug. *Courtesy of C.W.C.I. and St. Clere.* High

New Storks and *Spider Web* pitchers are displayed here with a S*ketching Bird* vase (all from the late 1930s). *Courtesy of C.W.C.I. and St. Clere.* Medium

Teaware, Cups and Saucers, and Bowls

Following shapes created by designers like Clarice Cliff and Susie Cooper, Carlton Ware clearly maintained its market share. Moreover, the creation of novelty items greatly increased the company's profit margins, keeping the firm viable for perhaps a decade longer than many would have thought.

Nursery Ware surfaced in most manufacturer's lines, and Carlton Ware was no exception. These 4-inch teapots came in white or yellow, each pattern shown here in a set. *Courtesy of C.W.C.I. and St. Clere.* NP

An *Explosions* teapot rests beside a *Floral Comets* vase. *Courtesy of C.W.C.I. and St. Clere.* High+ each

Reminiscent of Clarice Cliff, this
hand-painted, honey-glazed set is
called *Autumn Trees and Fern.*
Courtesy of C.W.C.I. and St. Clere.
Medium for set

A floral saucer from the late 1930s.
Courtesy of C.W.C.I. and St. Clere.
Low

Cups and saucers came in a variety of patterns from this 3-inch modern shaped cup to the abstract designs on the demitasse examples. The yellow and orange *Intersections* contrasts the green and black *Carré* (French for squares) and *Chevrons. Courtesy of C.W.C.I. and St. Clere.* Low for each

This *Rainbow Fans* demitasse set has an oriental flavor. Featured with a *Dahlia & Butterfly* 6-inch vase and a *Devil's Copse* design without the devil figure. *Courtesy of C.W.C.I. and St. Clere.* Low; *Butterfly* High+

This *Dovecote* novelty teapot was designed by Roger Michell and Danka Napiorkowska for Carlton Ware in the mid 1970s. *Courtesy of C.W.C.I. and St. Clere.* Low

King Tut designs begun to appear on ceramics after his tomb was opened in 1922. This bowl shows Carlton Ware's *King Tut* pattern and the mark. *Courtesy of C.W.C.I. and St. Clere.* Very High

Measuring 7.5" x 12" in length, this footed bowl is the *Scimitar* pattern from the early 1930s. *Courtesy of C.W.C.I. and St. Clere.* Very High

The *Red Devil* design on this triform footed bowl (9" in diameter) depicts the same pattern as the *Devil's Copse* but here the figure is included. *Courtesy of C.W.C.I. and St. Clere.* Very High+

A *Tyrolean Bands* pattern is displayed here on an 8.5" x 10.5" bowl. Bands were popular designs of the 1930s, yet compare this design with those by Susie Cooper. *Courtesy of C.W.C.I. and St. Clere.* Medium

Fruit acid has dissolved the orange enamel on this *Geometric Butterfly* bowl, resulting in the white colorway in the center. (Note the orange edges.) Shown on either side of the bowl is an orange *Moonlight Cameo* vase 3" in height and an *Orchard* pattern 4-inch vase. *Courtesy of C.W.C.I. and St. Clere.* Low for each (Medium for bowl with orange colorway intact)

Babylon was another popular pattern of the late 1930s. *Courtesy of C.W.C.I. and St. Clere.* Medium

By the late 1930s, Carlton Ware designs depicted more subtle colors. For example, the *Metropolis* design on a velox bowl (10.5" in diameter) indicates the interest in urban development. *Courtesy of C.W.C.I. and St. Clere.* High

The delicate designs of *Buttercup* appeared on a variety of wares and have a unique appeal. Low

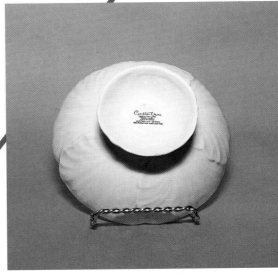

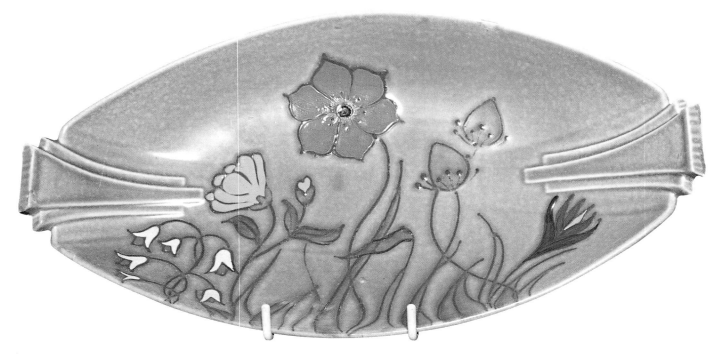

A floral design oblong bowl from the late 1930s. *Courtesy of C.W.C.I. and St. Clere.* Low

Miscellaneous

Everything from stylish vases of Oriental and Egyptian inspiration to novelty napkin rings and bells in figural shapes offer the collector an unusual source of collectibles. Embossed chocolate mugs contrast the temple jars, while crinoline ladies atop powder jars complement the vicar and ringmaster bells. Whichever way the collector chooses to amass items, Carlton Ware provides the unusual.

A very rare *Winter Scene* on a ginger jar. The leaping deer reminds one of the Susie Cooper deer. This piece is a design prototype and probably one of a kind, as the design was never manufactured. *Courtesy of C.W.C.I. and St. Clere.* Very Rare

This *Shabukin*, or river fish, 7.25-inch bowl unfortunately has a crack. The pattern coordinates nicely with the *Fairy* pattern on the 7-inch vase. *Courtesy of C.W.C.I. and St. Clere.* High

The oriental influence is quite clear on this 5.5-inch Fan vase and 8.25-inch temple jar of cobalt and gold. Note the Dog of Fo finial on the jar. *Courtesy of C.W.C.I. and St. Clere.* High to Very High

The enduring popularity of blue and white continues even today. Certainly, these designs were well received in the 1930s. The *Florabunda* ginger jar from the *Handcraft* range and the *Shamrock* must have delighted the consumer of the period. *Courtesy of C.W.C.I. and St. Clere.* Medium and Low respectively

The bands of *Medley* ran vertically as well as horizontally. These pieces range in size from the 4.5-inch lidded jar to the same size vase to the 5-inch powder jar. *Courtesy of C.W.C.I. and St. Clere.* Low

A 7-inch biscuit jar with a *New Chinese Bird & Cloud* and a vase with a *Crested Bird & Water Lily* express an oriental inspiration, popular in the 1920s. *Courtesy of C.W.C.I. and St. Clere.* Medium and High respectively

Lace Cap Hydrangea, 5" in height, and a cobalt *Fantasia* lidded jar illustrate the unusual use of floral designs. *Courtesy of C.W.C.I. and St. Clere.* Medium+

Another unusual floral cobalt design featured here on a biscuit jar. *Collection of Carole A. Berk, Ltd.* Very High

The 1920s design, *Flies,* actually represents moths rather than butterflies. The interior of the 3.5-inch blue bowl resembles the exterior of the 5.5-inch vase. *Courtesy of C.W.C.I. and St. Clere.* Medium

This *Orchid* piece somewhat resembles the pottery of Poole, while the *Geometrica* design is an unusual combination of shapes. The focal point of the squares attracts the eye even as the contrasting orange and black draw the eye up and down. The movement behind takes the eye around. *Courtesy of C.W.C.I. and St. Clere.* Medium

A floral 3.5-inch vase appears this time with an orange background. *Courtesy of Carole A. Berk, Ltd.* Medium

The *Persian* pattern and the *Temple* design from these 1920s vases indicate a widespread interest in other cultures, a trend which began in the last half of nineteenth-century in Britain. During this time period, with the expansion of the British empire, British pottery began to reflect a variety of traditional patterns. *Courtesy of C.W.C.I. and St. Clere.* Medium

Called *Carnival*, this 9.5-inch vase clearly reflects an Aztec influence. Reminiscent of Poole Pottery, the diagonal lines attract the eye to the side, while the circles carefully balance the pattern. *Courtesy of C.W.C.I. and St. Clere.* High

Following the tradition established by both Cliff and Cooper for using geometric shapes, Carlton Ware created this *Incised Square* and *Incised Diamond*. From the 1940s, this design makes use of orange in an interesting counterbalance. *Courtesy of C.W.C.I. and St. Clere.* High

This 10.5-inch vase exhibits the *Iris* design, an artistically well-planned design with its vertical lines moving the eye up and down. *Courtesy of C.W.C.I. and St. Clere.* High

Other floral designs include this *Peach Melba* on a 4.5-inch vase and a tube-lined *Marigold* on a 3.4-inch vase. The latter is reminiscent of Charlotte Rhead's designs. *Courtesy of C.W.C.I. and St. Clere.* Low

A *Monsoon* double-handled vase and the rippled effect of the *Stoneware* illustrate the softer colors used in the late 1930s. *Courtesy of C.W.C.I. and St. Clere.* Low

A display of some matt 1930s vases, including *Handcraft*, shown on an original Carlton Ware stand. *Courtesy of C.W.C.I. and St. Clere.* NP

The *King Tut* pattern appears here on an ashtray with a bust of the king on the inside. *Courtesy of C.W.C.I. and St. Clere.* High

The design on this 8-inch cocktail shaker from the 1920s is typical of the international influences on the ceramics of the period. *Courtesy of C.W.C.I. and St. Clere.* High

Listed only as "Mug and Cover" in the factory records, these floral embossed chocolate mugs stand 5" in height. *May Avenue, Antiquarius, London.* Low to Medium

The *Buttercup* pattern is seen here on a sugar shaker and a cruet set. *Courtesy of C.W.C.I. and St. Clere.* Medium

Buttercup also appeared in pink, as with this cruet set and condiment dish. However, the pattern is harder to find in pink. *May Avenue, Antiquarius, London.* Medium

A floral embossed leaf dish is shown here in its original box. *May Avenue, Antiquarius, London.* Low

A display of Carlton Ware with a floral embossed cheese dish in the center. *Courtesy of Beverly.* NP

The *Cottage Ware* pieces included a toast rack, cheese dish, and a cruet. *Courtesy of C.W.C.I. and St. Clere.* Low to Medium

This miscellaneous grouping includes a 6-inch candleholder of *Gazania*, a *Spangled Tree* 10.75-inch dish, and a 6.5-inch vase. *Courtesy of C.W.C.I. and St. Clere.* Medium to High

The detail of this 15.5-inch *Russian* pattern wall plaque by Carlton Ware highlights the intricate design of the pattern. *Courtesy of C.W.C.I. and St. Clere.* High+

The detail of another equally complex design on a wall plaque. *Courtesy of C.W.C.I. and St. Clere.*

Note the same figure for the body on both the designs of these powder bowls from the 1920s.
Courtesy of C.W.C.I. and St. Clere.
Medium

The figure on this powder bowl is arched to form the handle.
Courtesy of C.W.C.I. and St. Clere.
NP

Carlton Ware made some delightful figures, including these bride and groom ashtrays and these figural bells of the vicar, the ringmaster, and the bell boy.
Courtesy of C.W.C.I. and St. Clere.
Low to Medium

Limited editions of figures such as these made from old molds are for sale by the Carlton Ware Collectors International. *Courtesy of C.W.C.I. and St. Clere.* Low

This *Crinoline Lady* and the flower girl are both bells, while the dog Toby, the soldier, and the gazelle are napkin rings. *Courtesy of C.W.C.I. and St. Clere.* Low

Shown here is a charming grouping of Carlton Ware figures and nursery ware. *Courtesy of C.W.C.I. and St. Clere.* NP

Carlton Ware offered these charming animals: A *Glacielle Ware* dog (after the Sevres "Vin Saire" type of pottery) 7.5" in height; the lion cubs 5" in width; and the goose 8.25" in height. The rat is 7" in length and the penguin is 7" in height. The penguin appeared on the market only in black and white, but in the process of restoration this fellow's feet were mistakenly painted orange. *Courtesy of C.W.C.I. and St. Clere.* Low to Medium

Birds by Carlton Ware included the bird with blue, which is the centerpiece for a "floating bowl." *Courtesy of C.W.C.I. and St. Clere.* Low

Carlton Ware makes an interesting store display. *Courtesy of Beverly.* NP

Another Carlton Ware store display. *Courtesy of Beverly*. NP

Left, above, and right:
However one chooses to focus a collection, because of the variety available, Carlton Ware offers something for any collector: whether a beginning collector or an advanced one. Some collectors concentrate on a particular color, or a particular style, while others collect pieces from each range. *Courtesy of C.W.C.I. and St. Clere.* NP

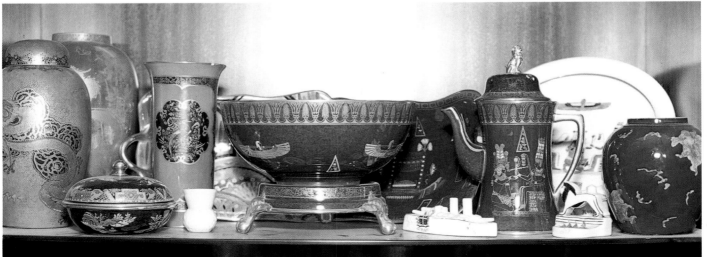

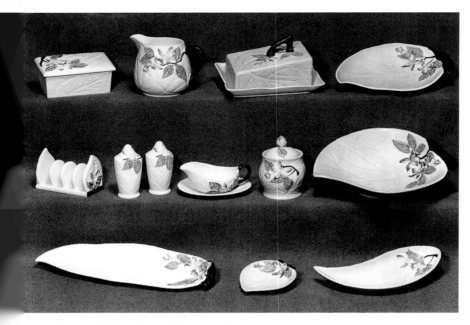

Carlton Ware reintroduced the floral and fruit embossed lines. Shown here is the *Apple Blossom* pattern as it was reintroduced. *Courtesy of C.W.C.I. and St. Clere.* NP

In Conclusion . . .

The twentieth-century designers like Clarice Cliff, Susie Cooper, Keith Murray, Charlotte Rhead, and those at the Carlton Works offer some of the most inventive patterns and shapes of any period in the history of ceramics. Perhaps this diversity accounts for the recent surge in popularity among these designers and their contemporaries. The Victorian manufacturers emulated wares of the seventeenth and eighteenth centuries with one revival after another, yet each revival exhibited its own technical innovations and creative adaptations.

Each new century seems to appreciate items from the preceding one. Today's collectors enjoy the diversity of nineteenth-century ceramics but are increasingly appreciative of the pottery of the twentieth century. The sheer variety of the Art Deco and Modernist ceramics chronicles for posterity a very important time in history. Collectors of these designs gain not only information about particular factories, but also perspective on the vast changes brought about by air travel, nuclear energy, and the space age.

Within the field of collecting Art Deco and Modernist ceramics, there is truly something for everyone!

Helen and Keith Martin, the owners of the *Carlton Ware Collectors International* and *St. Clere*, can't help but smile when surrounded by the bright, cheerful pieces of Carlton Ware!

Endnotes

Chapter One

Endnote citations are placed at the end of the discussions in all chapters.

1. Picasso Exhibit, High Museum of Art (Atlanta: February 14, 1998).
2. Richard Green and Des Jones, *The Rich Designs of Clarice Cliff* (Warwickshire: Rich Designs, 1995), p. 20.

Chapter Two

1. *Clarice Cliff* (Brighton: Brighton Museum & Art Gallery Exhibition Catalog, 1972), quoted in Howard Watson, *Collecting Clarice Cliff* (London: Kevin Francis Publishing, 1988), p. 11.
2. Leonard Griffin, *Taking Tea with Clarice Cliff* (London: Pavilion Books, 1996), p. 11, and Peter Wentworth-Shields and Kay Johnson, *Clarice Cliff* (London: O'deon, 1976), p. 13.
3. *British Pottery, An Illustrated Guide* (London: Barrie & Jenkins, 1974), quoted in Watson.
4. Green and Jones, p. 24.
5. Griffin & Louis K. and Susan Pear Meisel, *The Bizarre Affair* (New York: Harry N. Abrams, 1988), pp. 61-64.
6. Green and Jones, pp. 48-50.
7. Jane Hay, *Christie's Collectibles: Art Deco Ceramics* (Boston: Little, Brown and Company, 1996), p. 25.

Chapter Three

1. Andrew Casey, *Susie Cooper Ceramics: A Collector's Guide* (Warwickshire: Jazz Publications Limited, 1992), pp. 9-13.
2. Paul Niblett, *Hand-Painted: Gray's Pottery* (Stoke-on-Trent: City Museum and Art Gallery Exhibition Catalog, 1982), p. 7.
3. Bryn Youds, *Susie Cooper: An Elegant Affair* (London: Thames and Hudson Ltd., 1996), p. 15.
4. Casey, p. 23.

5. Casey, p. 31.
6. Marian Scott, "Susie Cooper," *The Gazette* (6 March, 1993), p. 120.
7. Kathy Niblett, Information for Introductory Panels (Stoke-on-Trent: City Museum and Art Gallery Exhibit for Susie Cooper's Eightieth Birthday) 29 October, 1982.

Chapter Four

1. Robert Reilly and George Savage, *The Dictionary of Wedgwood* (Suffolk: Antique Collectors' Clubs Ltd., 1980), p. 246.
2. Carole A. Berk, "Keith Murray: Simplicity and Practicality by Design," *The Antiques Journal* vol XVI, no. 3 (Sept 1997), pp. 28-29.

Chapter Five

1. Bernard Bumpus, *Charlotte Rhead: Potter & Designer* (London: Kevin Francis Publishing, 1987), pp. 9-12.
2. "Buyers' Notes," (1 February), p. 185, quoted in Cheryl Buckley, *Potters and Paintresses: Women Designers in the Pottery Industry 1870-1955* (Women's Press, 1990), p. 110.
3. John A. Bartlett, *British Ceramic Art, 1870 to 1940* (Atglen, PA: Schiffer Publishing Ltd., 1993), pp. 195-197.

Chapter Six

All of the information in this chapter was provided either directly or indirectly by Helen and Keith Martin, owners of the Carlton Ware Collectors International.

1. Personal interview, March 10, 1998; Helen Martin, "Carlton Ware, Part 1: 1890-1930s," *Antique Collecting* (March 1998), p. 15-19; and Helen Martin, "The Charm of Carlton Ware," *Antiques in the West Country* (February 1997), pp. 8-9.
2. Marshall P. Katz, "Walking Ware," *Antiques & Collecting* (December 1997), pp. 45, 52-55.

Index of Contributors

American Toby Jug Museum
917 Chicago Avenue
Evansville, Illinois 60202

Art Deco Originals
Halifax Antiques Centre
Queens Road Mills
Queens Road/Gibbet Street
Halifax HX1 4LR
England

Banana Dance
The Northcote Road Antiques Market
Unit 20, 155a Northcote Road
London, SW11 6QB
England
World Wide Web address: http://www.banana-dance.co.uk/banana.htm

Beverly
30 Church Street
London NW8 8EP
England

CARA Antiques
13-313 Summit Square Center
Langhorne, PA 19047

Carlton Ware Collectors International
P. O. Box 161
Sevenoaks, Kent TN15 6GA
England

Carole A. Berk, Ltd.
4918 Fairmont Avenue
Bethesda, Maryland 20814

Grandad's Attic
12 Marischal Street
Aberdeen AB1 2AJ
Scotland

Lattimore's Art Deco Directory
World Wide Web address: http://www.lattimore.co.uk/deco

Lorraine Donnelly Art Deco Ceramics
Unit 17, Lower Ground Floor
Georgian Village, Camden Passage
London N1
England
World Wide Web address:http://www.lattimore.co.uk/deco/donnelly

May Avenue
Antiquarius V13
131-141 Kings Road
Chelsea, London SW3 4PW
England
World Wide Web address: http://www.mayavenue.co.uk

Markov & Beedles
Sydney Street Antiques, Shop Unit 21
151 Sydney Street
Chelsea, London SW3 6NT
England

Plum's Emporium
107 Miranda Avenue
Toronto, Ontario M6B 3W8
Canada

Susie Cooper Ceramics
Alfies Antique Market
13-15 Church Street
London SE1 6ER
England

Witney & Airault Decorative Arts
The Lanes Gallery
32 Meeting House Lane
Brighton BN1 1HB
East Sussex, England
World Wide Web address: http://www3.mistral.co.uk/witair

Bibliography

Pottery Resources

Atterbury, Paul J., ed. *European Pottery and Porcelain*. New York: Mayflower Books, USA, 1979.

_____. "Collecting Clarice." *Homes & Gardens* (July 1985): 74-75.

Bartlett, John A. *British Ceramic Art 1870-1940*. Atglen, PA: Schiffer Publishing Ltd., 1993.

Battie, David, and Michael Turner. *The Guide to 19th and 20th Century Pottery*. Suffolk, England: Antique Collectors' Club Ltd., 1987. Reprint, 1990.

Berk, Carole A. "Bold, Beautiful Bizarre Ware: Early Clarice Cliff Pottery." *Antiques West News Magazine*. 17:5, (May 1997): 6-7.

_____. "Keith Murray: Simplicity and Practicality by Design." *The Antiques Journal*. 16:3, (Sept 1997): 28-29.

Blacker, J. F. *The A.B.C. of Collecting Old English Pottery*. London: Stanley Paul and Co.

British Art and Design before the War. Arts Council of Great Britain, 1979.

Buckley, Cheryl. *Potters and Paintresses: Women Designers in the Pottery Industry, 1870-1955*. London: Women's Press, 1990.

Bumpus, Bernard. *Charlotte Rhead: Potter & Designer*. London: Kevin Francis Publishing, 1987.

_____. "Cheerful Charlotte Rhead." *Antique Dealer & Collector* (Aug 1988): 46-48.

_____. "Pottery Designed by Charlotte Rhead." *Antique Collector* (Jan 1983): 60-62.

_____. *Rhead: Artists & Potters 1870-1950*. London: Geffrye Museum, 1986.

_____. "Tube-line Variations." *Antique Collector* (Dec 1985): 59-61.

Casey, Andrew. *Susie Cooper Ceramics: A Collectors Guide*. Warwickshire, England: Jazz Publications Limited, 1992.

Chaffers, William. *Collector's Handbook of Marks and Monograms on Pottery and Porcelain*. Los Angeles: Borden Publishing Company.

Charleston, Robert J., ed. *World Ceramics*. New York: The Hamlyn Publishing Group Ltd., 1968.

Clarice Cliff. Brighton Museum and Art Gallery Exhibition Catalog, 1972.

Clarice Cliff. Manchester City Art Gallery, 1993.

Collecting Susie Cooper. London: Francis Joseph Publications, 1994.

Cox, Warren E. *The Book of Pottery and Porcelain*, vol. I and II. New York: Crown Publishers, 1944.

Cushion, John P. *Animals in Pottery and Porcelain*. New York: Crown Publishers, 1974.

Cushion, John P., and William B. Honey. *Handbook of Pottery & Porcelain Marks*. 4th ed. London: Faber & Faber, 1980.

Eatwell, Ann. *Susie Cooper Productions*. London: Victoria and Albert Museum, 1987.

Field, Rachael. *MacDonald Guide to Buying Antique Pottery and Porcelain*. Radnor, PA: Wallace-Homestead Book Company, 1987.

Finer, Ann, and George Savage. *The Selected Letters of Josiah Wedgwood*. London: Cory, Adams and MacKay, 1965.

Fletcher, Neil. "Sixty Glorious Years: The Work of Susie Cooper, O.B.E." *Antique Collecting* (Oct 1984): 26-30.

Gilchrist, Brenda, gen. ed. *The Smithsonian Illustrated Library of Antiques: Pottery*. New York: Cooper-Hewitt Museum, 1981.

Godden, Geoffrey A. *The Concise Guide to British Pottery and Porcelain*. London: Barrie and Jenkins, 1973.

_____. *Encyclopedia of British Pottery and Porcelain Marks*. New York: Bonanza Books, 1964.

Goreley, Jean. *The Collector's Library: Wedgwood*. New York: Gramercy Publishing Co., 1950.

Green, Richard, and Des Jones. *The Rich Designs of Clarice Cliff*. Warwickshire, England: Rich Designs, 1995.

Griffin, Leonard and Louis K., and Susan Pear Meisel. *Clarice Cliff: The Bizarre Affair*. New York: Harry A. Abrams, 1988.

_____. *Taking Tea with Clarice Cliff*. London: Pavilion Books, 1996.

_____. *The Fantastic Flowers of Clarice Cliff*. http://www.banana-dance.co.uk/banana.htm (3 Feb. 1998).

Hartman, Urban. *Porcelain and Pottery Marks*. New York: privately published, 1943.

Haslom, Malcolm. *Connoisseur's Library: Pottery*. London: Orbis Publishing, 1972.

Hay, Jane. *Christie's Collectibles: Art Deco Ceramics*. Boston: Little, Brown and Company, 1996.

Hayward, Leslie. *Poole Pottery: Carter & Company and their Successors, 1873-1995*. Somerset, England: Richard Dennis, 1995.

Hopwood, Irene and Gordon. *The Shorter Connection: A. J. Wilkinson, Clarice Cliff, Crown Devon*. Somerset, England: Richard Dennis, 1992.

Jewitt, Llewellynn. *The Ceramic Art of Great Britain*. London: J. S. Virtue and Company, 1878; rev. 1883.

Jones, Joan. *Minton: The First Two Hundred Years of Design and Production*. Shrewsbury, England: Swan Hill Press, 1993.

Kovel, Ralph M. and Terry H. *Dictionary of Marks on Pottery and Porcelain*. New York: Crown Publishing, 1953.

_____. *New Dictionary of Marks: Pottery and Porcelain 1850 to the Present*. New York: Crown Publishing, 1986.

Lewis, Griselda. *Collector's History of English Pottery*. New York: Viking Press, 1969.

Little Romances of China. Syracuse, NY: privately printed for Onondaga Pottery Company, 1919.

Macht, Carol. *Classical Wedgwood Designs*. New York: Gramercy Publishing, 1957.

Martin, Helen. "Carlton Ware, Part 1: 1890-1930." *Antique Collecting* (March 1998): 15-19.

_____."The Charm of Carlton Ware." *Antiques of the West Country* (Feb 1997): 8-9.

_____ and Keith. Personal Interview (10 Mar. 1998).

McCready, Karen. *Art Deco and Modernist Ceramics*. London: Thames and Hudson Ltd., 1995.

McLaren, Graham. *Ceramics of the 1950s*. Pembrokeshire, England: Shire Publications, 1997.

Moore, N. Hudson. *The Old China Book including Staffordshire, Wedgwood, Lustre and Other English Pottery and Porcelain*. New York: Tudor Publishing Company, 1903.

Niblett, Kathy, ed. *Wedgwood of Etruria and Barlaston*, Stoke-on-Trent: City Museum and Art Gallery, 1980.

_____. "Obituaries/Gazette: Susie Cooper." *The Independence* (1 Aug 1995): 10.

Niblett, Paul. *Hand-Painted: Gray's Pottery*. Stoke-on-Trent: City Museum and Art Gallery, 1982. Reprint, 1983, 1987.

Paton, James. *Jugs: A Collector's Guide*. London: Souvenir Press Ltd., 1976.

Petersen, E. Paul and A. *Collector's Handbook to Marks on Porcelain and Pottery*. Green Farms, CT: Modern Books and Crafts, 1974.

Ray, Marcia. *Collectible Ceramics: An Encyclopedia of Pottery and Porcelain for the American Collector*. New York: Crown Publishing, 1974.

Ramsey, L. G., ed. *The Connoisseur New Guide to Antique English Pottery, Porcelain and Glass*. New York: E. P. Dutton, 1961.

Reilly, Robin, and George Savage. *The Dictionary of Wedgwood*. Suffolk, England: Antique Collectors' Club Ltd., 1980.

Rhodes, Daniel. *Clay and Glazes for the Potter*. New York: Chilton Book Company, 1957. Reprint, 1968.

Savage, George. *Ceramics for the Collector: An Introduction to Pottery and Porcelain*. London: Salisbury Square, 1949.

Scott, Marian. "Susie Cooper." *The Gazette* (6 March 1993): 120-123.

Snodin, Su. "Susie Cooper: Diverse Designer." *Antique Collector* (Aug 1982): 53-55.

Spours, Judy. *Art Deco Tableware: British Domestic Ceramics 1925-1939*. New York: Rizzoli International Publications, 1988.

Steele, William O. "The Curious Case of Cherokee Clay." *Historical Review and Antique Digest* (Winter 1974): 11-13.

Stirling, Robert. "Carlton Ware: Naturalistic Patterns of the 1930s and 1940s." *Antique Collectors' Club,* May 1984.

"Susie Cooper." *Antique Collector* (8 Nov 1993): 42-44.

"The China Syndrome." *Crafts* (Sept/Oct 1992): 22-25.

Thorn, C. Jordan. *Handbook of Old Pottery and Porcelain Marks*. New York: Tudor Publishing Company, 1947.

Wakefield, Hugh. *Victorian Pottery*. New York: Thomas Nelson and Sons, 1962.

Watson, Howard. *Collecting Clarice Cliff*. London: Kevin Francis Publishing, 1988.

_____ and Pat. *Collecting Art Deco Ceramics*. London: Kevin Francis Publishing, 1993.

_____. *Collecting Art Deco Ceramics*. 2nd. ed. London: Francis Joseph Publications, 1997.

_____. *The Clarice Cliff Colour Price Guide*. London: Francis Joseph Publications, 1995.

_____. "Commercial Courage." *Antique Dealer and Collectors Guide* (April 1988): 24-27.

_____. *The Colourful World of Clarice Cliff*. London: Kevin Francis Publishing, 1992.

_____ Pat. "The Elusive Charlotte Rhead." *Antique*

& Collectors Fayre 2:1 (July 1987): 6.

Weatherill, L. The Pottery Trade & North Staffordshire. Manchester: University Press, 1971.

Wentworth-Shields, Peter, and Kay Johnson. Clarice Cliff. London: L'Odeon, 1976.

Whipp, R. "Women Pottery Workers of Staffordshire and Trade Unions." Unpublished Master's Thesis, Warwick University, 1980.

Williams, Peter. Wedgwood: A Collector's Guide. Radnor, PA: Wallace-Homestead Book Company, 1992.

Woodhouse, A. Elegance & Utility. Stoke-on-Trent: Josiah Wedgwood & Sons Ltd., 1978.

Youds, Bryn. Susie Cooper: An Elegant Affair. London: Thames and Hudson Ltd., 1996.

General Resources

Battersby, Martin. The Decorative Thirties. London: Studio Vista, 1969.

Bond, Harold Lewis. An Encyclopedia of Antiques. New York: Tudor Publishing Company, 1945.

Bouillon, Jean-Paul. Art Deco 1900-1940. New York: Rizzoli International Publications, 1988.

British Art and Design 1900-1960. London: Victoria and Albert Museum, 1984.

Bumpus, Judith. Impressionist Gardens. New York: Barnes and Noble, 1990.

Chefs-D'Oeuvres de l'Art Grands Peintres: Renoir. Paris: Hachette.

Carpenter, Rhys. The Esthetic Basis of Greek Art. Bloomington, IN: Indiana University Press, 1959.

Christensen, Erwin O. The History of Western Art. New York: The New American Library, 1959.

Cogniat, Raymond. Chagall. New York: Crown Publishers, 1978.

Cortenova, Giorgio. Picasso: The Works of Pablo Picasso. New York: Smithmark Publishers, 1991.

Costantino, Marcia. Paul Gauguin. New York: Barnes and Noble, 1994.

Davenport, Millia. The Book of Costume, vol. 1. New York: Crown Publishers, 1948.

Denvir, Bernard. The Thames and Hudson Ltd. Encyclopedia of Impressionism. London: Thames and Hudson Ltd., 1990.

Drepperd, Carl W. Victorian: The Cinderella of Antiques. Garden City, NY: Doubleday and Company, 1950.

Duncan, Alastair. American Art Deco. New York: Harry N. Abrams, 1986.

_____. Art Deco. London: Thames and Hudson Ltd., 1988.

_____. The Encyclopedia of Art Deco. New York: Dutton, 1988.

Durozoi, Gerard. Matisse. New York: Portland House, 1989.

Gaston, Mary Frank. Collector's Guide to Art Deco. Paducah, KY: Collector Books, 1989.

Gaunt, William. English Painting. London: Thames and Hudson Ltd., 1964. Reprint, 1988.

Gere, Charlotte, and Michael Whiteway. Nineteenth Century Design: From Pugin to Mackintosh. New York: Harry N. Abrams, 1994.

Gimferrer, Pere. Toulouse-Lautrec. New York: Rizzoli International Publications, 1990.

Gowing, Sir Lawrence, gen. ed. A History of Art. New York: Barnes and Noble, 1983; rev. 1995.

Grosline, Douglas. What People Wore: A Visual History of Dress from Ancient Times to Twentieth Century America. New York: Bonanza Books, 1951.

Hardy, William. A Guide to Art Nouveau Style. London: Chartwell Books, 1986. Reprint, 1988.

Hartt, Frederick. History of Italian Renaissance Art. New York: Harry N. Abrams, 1969.

Heinrich, Christoph. Monet. New York: Barnes and Noble, 1996.

Herbert, Robert L. Impressionism: Art, Leisure, and Parisian Society. New Haven: Yale University Press, 1988.

Hibbert, Christopher. The Horizon Book of Daily Life in Victorian England. New York: American Heritage Publishing Company, 1975.

Hillier, Bevis. Art Deco. London: Studio Vista, 1968.

_____. The World of Art Deco. New York: E. P. Dutton, 1971.

Hyman, Kay. Picasso and Cubism. North Dighton, MA: JG Press, 1994.

Jacobs, Jay. The Color Encyclopedia of World Art. New York: Crown Publishers, 1975.

Jenkins, Dorothy H. A Treasure in the Junk Pile. New York: Crown Publishers, 1963.

Langbaum, Robert. The Victorian Age. Chicago: Academy Publishing, 1969.

Machlis, Joseph. The Enjoyment of Music: An Introduction to Perceptive Listening. 4th ed. New York: W. W. Norton and Company, 1977.

Miller, R. Craig. Modern Design in the Metropolitan Museum of Art 1890-1990. New York: Harry N. Abrams, 1990.

Miró. Ed. José María Faerna. New York: Harry N. Abrams, 1995.

Mobelier et Décoration. Paris: Editions Edmund Honor, 1929, 1939.

Munro, Eleanor C. The Encyclopedia of Art. New York: Golden Press, 1961.

Neret, Gilles. The Arts of the Twenties. New York: Rizzoli International Publications, 1986.

Perry, Marvin, et al. Western Civilization: Ideas, Poli-

tics and Society. 4th ed. vol 2. Boston: Houghton, Mifflin Company, 1992.

Pool, Daniel. *What Jane Austen Ate and Charles Dickens Knew: From Fox Hunting to Whist—The Facts of Daily Life in Nineteenth-Century England*. New York: Simon and Schuster, 1993.

Prall, Stuart E., and David Harris Willson. *A History of England: 1603 to the Present*. 4th ed. vol. 2. Ft. Worth: Holt, Rinehart and Winston, 1991.

Reyna, Ferdinando. *A Concise History of Ballet*. New York: Grosset and Dunlap, 1964.

Ramié, Georges. *Ceramics of Picasso*. Barcelona: Ediciones Poligrafa, 1985.

Robinson, Walter. *Instant Art History: From Cave Art to Pop Art*. New York: Fawcett Columbine, 1995.

Scarlett, Frank, and Marjorie Townley. *Arts Dècoratifs 1925: A Personal Recollection of the Paris Exhibition*. London: Academy Editions, 1975.

Smith, Paul. *Interpreting* Cézanne. New York: Stewart, Tabori and Chang, 1996.

Tobias, J. J. *Urban Crime in Victorian England*. New York: Schocken Books, 1967.

Trevelyn, G. M. *English Social History: A Survey of Six Centuries—Chaucer to Queen Victoria.* London: Longman Group, Ltd., 1944.

Weber, Eva. *Art Deco*. New York: Smithmark Publishers, 1989.

_____. *Art Deco in America*. New York: Exeter Books, 1985.

World of Art Deco, The. Minneapolis, MN: Minneapolis Institute of Art, 1971.

Youngs, Grederic A., Jr., et al. *The English Heritage*. 2nd ed. Arlington Heights, IL: Forum Press, 1988.

Index